The Netwise Investor

Free Investment Resources On The Internet

Jordan Cohen

The Joralis Group

The Joralis Group
22575 Maywood Road
Farmington Hills, MI 48335-3941

mailbox@joralis.com (e-mail)

http://www.joralis.com
http://www.netwiseinvestor.com

Cover Design by Tiffany Butler

Library of Congress Card Number: 97-70478
Cohen, Jordan
The Netwise Investor, Free Investment Resources on the Internet
Includes Index
ISBN 0-9657299-5-8

Printed in the United States of America
10 9 8 7 6 5 4 3 2 1

Contents

Using This Book

Welcome

The less money you spend on figuring out where to invest your money, the more money you'll have to invest. With that in mind, *The Netwise Investor* will help you save time, energy and money by pointing you to specific locations on the internet where you can find valuable investment information that's free.

Send your comments by e-mail to: comments@netwiseinvestor.com.

What's Inside

This book is a power tool for people who want to spend their time using investment and financial information, rather than searching for it. Here is an explanation of how this guide is organized, and how to start using it.

Internet Access—Getting It, And Making Sure You've Got The Right Deal There are a couple of questions you should ask yourself about your internet access service before you begin your career as a Netwise Investor. You'll find these questions, along with the names and numbers of some internet access providers, in the section entitled **Internet Access**.

Becoming A Netwise Investor—Where To Start If you're unsure about where to begin, look at the section entitled **Where To Start**. This uses resources already available on the web to take you through a tutorial on the basics of personal investing. Even if you have some experience as an investor, you may want to take yourself through this section to confirm that your investment strategy has a sound foundation.

Find Things Fast With The Power Index Next, take a look at the **Power Index**, which allows you to look at the web sites covered by this book in terms of the specific topics or types of free information that are available at each site. The Power Index allows you to quickly narrow your focus to a few sites that have exactly the type of information that you're seeking, rather than wandering around general financial sites hoping to stumble upon the information.

For example, let's say you explore all of the sites in the Where To Start section, but you still want more of the same. In that case, look in the Power Index under "Getting Started." The Power Index is also the perfect place to look when you're searching for a particular piece of information about a potential investment, such as a company's Market Cap or Net Profit Margin.

Use The Power Index With The Web Site Summaries When you find a site in the Power Index that interests you, look up the summary of that site in the **Web Site Summaries** section. The site summary will serve as your roadmap when you visit the site online, helping you move swiftly to the area of the site that contains the information you want.

The site summaries are listed alphabetically by name. Each summary provides you with the site's URL address (the location you will enter in your browser to go to that web site). Below that appears a list of the Power Index subjects covered by that particular web site. This is followed by a narrative of the site's contents. To help you navigate the site, headings in the narrative will usually correspond to the names of areas in the site, and specific hyperlinks you may want to follow will be <u>underlined</u> (which is how most browsers will display the links when you are viewing the actual web site).

Other Stuff A few other sections of this book will give you a jump start in various areas that might interest you. **Quick & Dirty Stock Research** is, well, self-explanatory. **Newsgroups** will help you connect to a free-wheeling area of the internet where ideas, rumors and a lot of other things fly about with relative abandon, and you are welcome to join in. **Net Brokers** will help you find your brokerage firm, or a new firm, and tell you which firms offer stock trading over the internet. Add to these one more member of the self-explanatory club: **Offline—Things A Stock Broker Can Give You For Free**.

A Reminder About Information On The Internet

There is one thing in common between just about every piece of free information you will find on the internet: it doesn't come with a warranty. This does not mean you can't find useful information on the net. On the contrary, the vast majority of investment information you will come across will be accurate. However, you should always maintain a healthy dose of skepticism by asking yourself some simple questions:

- √ **Does this information make sense?**
- √ **Can I confirm this information from another source?**
- √ **What is the agenda of the person providing the information?**

Remember that everyone who posts information for free access on the internet has a reason for placing it there. The information provider might be an individual investor who is merely trying to share information she has learned with others (which certainly embodies the spirit of the internet). Some are governmental agencies who are fulfilling their mandate to make information available to the public (some reluctantly, some enthusiastically).

Some companies provide as much free information as possible to encourage you to visit their web sites, then earn money through selling web advertisements that you view as you navigate their sites. These are referred to as advertiser-supported sites. Some information providers sell space for public companies to post press releases that might be of interest to investors—the thing to remember here is that the press releases are written by the companies themselves, not by independent journalists. Other information providers give some information away for free in the hopes that you will purchase additional information from them.

None of these agendas are bad, and all of these agendas result in making information available to you for free. As with every other medium of communication, though, a person's agenda will tend to affect his message. For example, a consumer report comparing automobiles will be quite different from an auto company's sales brochure for a single automobile.

Remind yourself to stay aware of the difference between advice, opinions and facts. Take what you can from the net, but don't take everything at face value.

Web Sites That Require Registration And User Login

Some of the web sites reviewed in this book require registration in order to access all of the free information available at the site. During registration, you may be required to choose a username and a password. Since you won't be allowed to choose a username that is already in use at the site, and since you may want to login to several free sites that require registration, it will be much easier if you're able to use the same username and password at every site. To achieve this, try using a name that's more likely to be unique. For example, "jsmith" may already be in use at one or more sites, so try using "janetsmi" as a Login. You'll be able to use the same name at the most sites if your username is no more than 8 letters. The more often you're able to use the same Login, the fewer names you'll have to remember.

Internet Access

Internet Service Providers

If you use the internet as an investment tool, you're going to find yourself spending a lot of time on the net accessing information. Therefore, there are 2 important questions you should ask yourself. The first is:

√ **How much does my internet service provider charge for *unlimited* access?**

As you'll see in this book, there is an enormous amount of useful free information on the internet. However, if you're paying by the hour to access this free information, a great bargain can quickly turn into a great big bill from your internet service provider. With that in mind, listed below are a few internet service providers that offer unlimited access plans with no setup charges. These are all major players in the internet access game, and any one of them should be able to meet your basic needs for net access. However, this is not a recommendation of their services. Check for yourself to see the particular benefits offered by each company, and don't be afraid to change providers if you're unhappy with the service you're getting.

Provider	Monthly Cost	Phone	Web Site
AOL	$19.95	(800) 827-6364	http://www.aol.com
AT&T	$19.95	(800) 967-5363	http://www.att.com
MCI	$19.95	(800) 550-0927	http://www.mci.com
NetCom	$19.95	(800) 638-2661	http://www.netcom.com
Sprynet	$19.95	(800) 447-2971	http://www.sprynet.com

Don't forget to check out other service providers as well, including local and regional companies that may offer even better prices and package deals. For example, regional service provider FlashNet (http://www.flash.net) offers a rate of $14.95 per month (with a $35 setup fee), and offers an even lower rate for those willing to pay for an entire year in advance.

The second important question you should ask about your internet service is:

√ **Am I making a local phone call to access the internet?**

It's no good feeling smug about paying a flat rate for internet access if your local phone company is charging you by the minute. It's easy to double check on this. Find out what access number you'll be using when you dial in to your service provider, then call your local telephone operator and confirm that your access number is truly a local call for you.

Hardware

Where computer hardware is concerned, newer and faster always seem to be better. However, that doesn't mean an old computer won't do fine navigating the most interesting investment site you'll find on the World Wide Web. In general, your minimum hardware needs are going to be determined by the software you will use on your computer. In the case of internet access, your software usually will be provided by your internet service provider. Before you sign up with an internet service provider, ask them what the minimum hardware requirements are to run their software. As long as your computer runs their internet software, you'll do fine.

It's worth saying a word about modems, though. When you move to a new page or web site, that information needs to be downloaded through your modem. The faster your modem is, the faster you'll be able to move between web pages and web sites. If you have any choice in the matter, use at least a 14.4 Kbps modem; a 28.8 Kbps modem is even better, and anything faster than that will make you the envy of your friends.

Software

Internet software is usually provided by your internet service provider. However, you may have the option of using different browsers with your internet access software. If this is the case, you'll probably be happiest with either of these browser programs: Netscape's Navigator or Microsoft's Internet Explorer. That's because many web sites today, including financial sites, are being designed to look best when viewed with one of these browsers. As far as the browser battle goes, Netscape is on top for now, but Microsoft is starting to breath down Netscape's neck. For accessing investment sites, either browser will work fine. Once you're on the net, you can download the latest version of Navigator from Netscape's homepage (http://home.netscape.com), and Internet Explorer is available free at Microsoft's homepage (http://www.microsoft.com).

About The Internet

The instructions you receive from your internet service provider should enable you to get onto the internet and use a browser program to access the graphical pages on the World Wide Web. That's all you need to know to get started using this book. If you want to learn even more about the internet, use your browser to visit Internet 101 (http://www.sisna.com/users/scotting) to learn about safe surfing, web browsers, chat, online shopping, e-mail, locating software, avoiding viruses and newsgroups; or try Microsoft Network's Internet Tutorial (http://www.msn.com/tutorial/default.html).

Where To Start

> "What you invest in is the last decision. The first decision is: what do you want your investments to do for you; how much can you add to your investments over the years; what kind of diversification should you have for the risk level you are willing to bear (because the greater the diversification, the less the risk). The longer the investment is held, the better the chance for success. Ask yourself how you plan to monitor your investments. How will you choose your investments—using the advice of another, or by making your own selection? Invest over a long period of time even if you have a large lump sum to start with—never invest all of your money at once."
>
> Advice from a stock broker to his son

If you have a firm idea of what your information needs are, feel free to skip right to the Power Index to find out which sites have exactly what you need. However, if you'd like, this section will give you a small guided tour to help you get started. When you visit a site listed in this section, refer to the full site summary in the Web Site Summaries section of this book; this will make it easier to find the specific tool or article that you're seeking.

Once you've finished with this section, if you'd like to explore more of the same, look in the Power Index at the sites listed under Getting Started.

Start Here

Investing is a serious endeavor, but that doesn't mean you're not allowed to smile once in a while. With that in mind, make your first stop at:

The Motley Fool
http://www.fool.com

Don't let the name fool you (sorry about the pun)—The Motley Fool is serious about investing. Start by clicking on The 13 Steps, which leads to the section called The 13 Steps To Investing Foolishly (when they say foolish, they really mean smart). The articles here discuss the first steps of investing, such as getting your personal finances in order and choosing your first broker. You'll also read about the Fools' investment strategy. While you certainly don't have to adopt their strategy as your own, it's good to start thinking in terms of following a strategy in investing. While you're there, you might also drop in on The Motley Fool's School, which has articles on additional topics.

Next, take a look at this web site:

Individual Investor Services
http://www.investor.nasd.com

Individual Investor Services is part of the National Association of Securities Dealers. Drop in on their Investor Training section. Under Taking Charge of Your Finances, you'll find articles on: An Introduction to Investing; Investment Options; Assessing Your Current Finances; and Setting Objectives and Goals.

Get A Stock Quote & Set Up A Virtual Portfolio

Now that you're feeling comfortable with some of the basics of investing, you may feel compelled to rush out and buy that hot stock that you just know is going to rise. Don't do it. Instead, get the latest quote on the stock. Go to:

Quote.com's FastQuote
http://fast.quote.com/fq/quotecom/quote

Bookmark this page for easy access in the future (it's much faster to go to this page directly than going to Quote.com's homepage and maneuvering through the menus). In this section you can get the latest quote for your hot stock, and view historical charts as well. Now that you know what the stock is selling for, satisfy your urge to buy it, but without spending any money. Go to:

Research Magazine/InvestorNet
http://www.researchmag.com

Research will let you create virtual portfolios that you can return to whenever you wish. Create a "Watch List" portfolio (click on Watch List on the navigation bar at the top of the homepage), and whenever you see a stock that interests you, pretend to "buy" it at the current market price and place it in your Watch List. From then on, you can return to your portfolio at any time and see how well your virtual investments are doing. You can also view stock charts that include Research's technical analysis of how a stock is likely to perform in the future. Research provides information on specific mutual funds and specific companies so you can start thinking in terms of evaluating investments.

Examine Your Personal Finances

Now that you've gotten your feet wet and you know how to get quotes and start a portfolio, it's time to turn your focus inward and take a good hard look at yourself. One piece of advice you'll see repeatedly offered to new investors is that the first step to a true investment plan is getting your personal finances in order. Start by figuring out your net worth and cash flow. Visit:

Eanalytics
http://www.e-analytics.com

Eanalytics has worksheets you can print (or copy to your word processor) and fill out on your own. Under Financial Planning, you'll find the Net Worth Worksheet, which will help you add up your assets and liabilities to give you a better picture of your financial condition. The Cash Flow Worksheet will help you figure out your total income and compare it to your total expenses. These worksheets are very helpful because they break down these broad concepts into specific categories, making your task easier since all you have to do is fill in the blanks. While you're there, look under Insurance and Retirement Planning and fill out the How Much Life Insurance Do You Need Worksheet (it will probably take a little research on your personal benefits to answer some of the questions on this worksheet).

For many new investors, getting your personal finances in order means cutting credit card debt. This is because the interest you earn on your investments rarely will be as high as the interest you're paying on your credit card debt, so getting rid of that debt can be the fastest way to improve your financial picture. Go to:

Bank Rate Monitor
http://www.bankrate.com

Bank Rate Monitor will give you suggestions on how to cut your credit card debt. Look under Get The Rates for the best rates on Credit Cards and see whether you should switch credit card companies. While you're there, you can also check out savings rates in your local area to see if you can get more for your money by switching to a bank that's paying higher interest rates.

Your Financial Goals And Investment Personality

Now that you have a decent picture of your current financial situation, you should take a look at where you're hoping to end up, or more specifically, how much money you'll need when you get there. To assist you, a number of sites have various "calculators"—you enter specific information about yourself, and the calculator will perform the math for you and give you the results. To figure out how much money you'll need for retirement, or how much you'll need to pay for a child's education, go to:

Fidelity Investments
http://www.fid-inv.com

Click on Personal Investing, then on Tools. Fidelity's Retirement Planning Calculator will help you chart where you are and where you want to be when you retire, then tell you whether you're on track to reach your goals. The Fidelity College Cost Calculator also allows you to order a free College Savings Plan Kit by mail.

You should also think about your investment personality. The most important aspect of your investment personality is your risk tolerance. In general, the higher the return an investor seeks from an investment, the higher the risk he or she must be willing to accept. You should never make an investment if you're not comfortable with the level of risk of that investment. Fidelity Investments has a Savings Personality quiz that will take your answers and compare them to others. To take an even closer look at yourself, go to:

Prudential Securities
http://www.prusec.com

Under Life's Financial Concerns, PruSec's investment Personality Quiz will ask you some tough questions about yourself (don't worry, the quiz is anonymous), but it will give you a pretty good indication of where you fall on the risk tolerance curve.

The Vanguard Group (http://www.vanguard.com) also has an Investment Personality Profile to help you determine your risk tolerance. Enter the Retirement Center, then follow Planning for Retirement, then How to Develop an Investment Strategy. Their risk tolerance calculator is under Determine Your Risk Tolerance.

Remember, all of the above sites are starting points. Your interests and concerns will shape your research and your investment strategy. From here, follow the paths that prove to be the most interesting and valuable to you. Refer to the Power Index in this book for additional subject areas that interest you.

Mutual Funds

As you begin to consider individual investments, mutual funds will probably be high on your list. Mutual funds are often chosen as initial investments by individual investors because funds generally offer greater diversification (and therefore lesser risk) than an individual stock. If you didn't check out AAII's mutual fund area when you were there, take a second look (http://www.aaii.org). Next, drop in on the folks at:

NETworth
http://networth.galt.com

NETworth's mutual fund area has a great deal of information, including lists of top-performing mutual funds, fund profiles from Morningstar and a glossary of mutual fund terms.

Introductory information on mutual funds can also be found at Quote.com's web site (http://www.quote.com/mutual_funds/tutorial/index.html).

Stocks, Corporate SEC Filings & EDGAR

You'll be learning a lot about stocks as you go along, but this might be a good time to learn about the financial information found in corporate SEC filings.

Many companies have been providing their SEC filings in electronic form for some time. However, since May 1996, all public companies have been required to provide their corporate SEC filings in electronic form so they can be added to the SEC's EDGAR (Electronic Data Gathering and Retrieval) database. As an investor, you'll be especially interested in 10-Q Quarterly Reports and 10-K Annual Reports. Search the actual EDGAR database for filings of specific companies at:

NYU EDGAR
http://edgar.stern.nyu.edu

Exploring And Searching

If you're exploring a particular topic and you've exhausted the information available at the sites covered in this guide, there are still options available to you. First, many of the sites covered here offer links to even more related web sites that may have information that will be helpful to you. Second, don't be afraid to perform an old-fashioned search of the net. Netscape's web site makes a number of web search engines available to you from one simple menu (go to http://home.netscape.com, then click on Net Search). One of these tools is Digital Equipment Corporation's powerful AltaVista™ engine, which you can find at http://altavista.digital.com.

The Most Common Investment Mistakes

Before you dive in, you might benefit from a few nuggets of conventional wisdom. Here they are—the most common investment errors you can make.

Not getting the facts
Following fads in stocks
Jumping from investment to investment
Buying on tips
Buying only speculative or cyclical stocks
Reaching for high yields
Buying only low-priced issues
Failing to take a loss
Not having patience

If you want to see some more common mistakes investors make, take a look at Prudential Securities' own list of nine common investment mistakes to avoid (http://www.prusec.com/eqmist.htm).

Quick & Dirty Stock Research

Okay. You've worked your way through the Where To Start section of this book. You've given yourself an introduction to investing principles. You've examined your personal finances, your financial goals and your personal tolerance for risk.

Eventually, you're going to want to get information about a specific stock. Perhaps you'll read an interesting article in the newspaper, or even get a "hot stock tip" from a friend (who may or may not know anything about the company). This section will point you to a few resources you can use to get a "quick and dirty" picture of a particular company's stock, which will often be enough to determine whether the stock merits serious consideration as an investment, and further research.

Infoseek—Quotes & Charts

First, find out where the stock is now, and where the stock has been. Go to:

Infoseek
http://www.infoseek.com

Click on Smart Info: Stocks/Companies. Enter the stock symbol (or Look it up if you don't know it). Infoseek will provide you with a quote for the stock, as well as daily, weekly and monthly charts so you can get an idea of where the stock has been trading in the past.

Research Magazine/InvestorNet—Technical Analysis

Now that you've looked at the stock charts, take advantage of someone else's analysis. Drop in on:

Research Magazine/InvestorNet
http://www.researchmag.com

Enter your stock symbol and click on the Go to Ticker button. Next, choose Stock Summary to view a 52-week chart along with a prediction of how the stock will behave in the future, based purely on technical analysis. This screen also has earnings information for the company.

Stockprofiles.com—Company Snapshot

Get a snapshot report on the company. Go to:

Stockprofiles.com
http://www.stockprofiles.com

Click on Snapshot Reports and retrieve the company's stock report. The report will give you basic information about the company such as the Market Cap, the P/E Ratio and the Total Debt/Equity ratio. If you're unsure about any of these terms, look them up at one of the sites listed under Glossaries in the Power Index.

PCQuote—News

Read recent news stories and news releases concerning the company. Go to:

PC Quote
http://www.pcquote.com

Enter the stock symbol on the homepage, and when you retrieve the quote, click on Latest News to see recent headlines. The full text of each story is available by clicking on the headline.

NYU EDGAR—Corporate SEC Filings

Search the SEC's electronic database for corporate filings by the company at:

NYU EDGAR
http://edgar.stern.nyu.edu

Pay special attention to 10-Q Quarterly Reports and 10-K Annual Reports. Since they are filed with the SEC, these reports tend to be more evenhanded than press releases.

General Search

Wrap up your quick and dirty examination of the stock by doing a general search on the company name or the names of its products or services. This may give you a better idea of how the company is perceived in the marketplace, who its competitors are, or other information that you may not have anticipated finding. Use your favorite search engine or try Alta Vista (http://altavista.digital.com) or HotBot (http://www.hotbot.com).

Netwise Tidbit

Thomson Investors Network
http://www.thomsoninvest.net

Register as a guest for access to the news room and personalized portfolio feature.

Newsgroups

Newsgroups, also called usenet newsgroups, are the internet's version of bulletin boards where anyone can post a message. There are a large number of newsgroups out there, but your internet service provider may limit the newsgroups that are available to you.

Since anyone can post a message to a newsgroup, or respond to someone else's message, newsgroups tend to have a free-for-all atmosphere. In between the sales pitches, outright lies and off-topic or generally useless postings, you will also find honest people asking and answering questions of mutual interest to the newsgroup's subscribers. Dig in, have fun, but don't take anything you read too seriously without confirming it elsewhere.

To learn how to access newsgroups, refer to the instructions accompanying your internet access software.

Before you jump in and post your first message to a newsgroup, you should know that many bulk e-mailers surf the newsgroups looking for new names to add to their mailing lists. As a result, posting messages to a newsgroup will result in an increase in the amount of junk e-mail you receive.

Here are a number of newsgroups that relate to investing:

- alt.invest
- alt.invest.penny-stocks
- alt.invest.technical-analysis.omega
- misc.invest.canada
- misc.invest.financial-plan
- misc.invest.futures
- misc.invest.marketplace
- misc.invest.misc
- misc.invest.mutual-funds
- misc.invest.options
- misc.invest.stocks
- misc.invest.technical

Brokerage Firms On The Internet

The number of brokerage firms with a presence on the internet is growing. Some offer internet-based trading, and some don't. Here's a list to get you started. If a broker allows its customers to execute trades over the internet, the price of an average stock trade is also listed. You may not want to go by trade price alone when picking a broker. Find out as much as you can about a broker and its account services before choosing. For more general information on choosing a broker, visit AAII (http://www.aaii.org) and Individual Investor Services (http://www.investor.nasd.com).

A.G. Edwards http://www.agedwards.com
Alex Brown & Son http://www.alexbrown.com
Amer. Express Financial Direct http://www.americanexpress.com/direct
Net Trades: $26.95 + $.005 per share
Aufhauser & Co. http://www.aufhauser.com
Net Trades: $22.50
B.C. Ziegler http://www.ziegler.com
Baker & Co. http://www.bakernyse.com
Ceres Securities http://www.ceres.com
Net Trades: $18
CompuTEL Securities http://www.rapidtrade.com
Net Trades: $16.50/$21.50 for limit orders
Cowen & Co. http://www.cowen.com
Cutter & Co. Brokerage http://www.stocktrader.com
Net Trades: $55 avg.
Datek http://www.datek.com
Net Trades: $9.99
eBroker http://www.ebroker.com
Net Trades: $12
Edward Jones http://www.edwardjones.com
E*Trade http://www.etrade.com
Net Trades: $14.95/$19.95 for NASDAQ orders
Ferris, Baker Watts http://www.fbw.com
Freedom Investments Inc http://www.tradeflash.com
Investex Securities Group, Inc. http://www.investexpress.com
Net Trades: $13.95, $17.95 for limit orders
Janney Montgomery Scott http://www.janneys.com
JRP Securities, Inc http://pawws.com/Jrp
Net Trades: (coming soon)
Jack White & Co. http://pawws.com/Broker/Jwc
Net Trades: $25
Legg Mason http://www.leggmason.com

Lombard Institut. Brokerage http://www.lombard.com
Net Trades: $14.95/$19.95 for limit orders
Merrill Lynch http://www.ml.com
Olde Discount Corp http://www.oldediscount.com
National Discount Brokers http://www.ndb.com
Net Trades: $14.75/$19.75 for limit orders
Net Investor http://pawws.com/Broker/How
Net Trades: $29.00 plus 1.5 cents per share
Pacific Brokerage Services, Inc. http://www.tradepbs.com
Net Trades: $15
PC Financial Network Http://www.pcfn.com
Net Trades: $39.95
PaineWebber http://www.painewebber.com
Piper Jaffray http://www.piperjaffray.com
Prudential Securities http://www.prusec.com
Quick & Reilly http://www.quick-reilly.com
Net Trades: $26.75
Regal Discount Brokers http://www.regaldiscount.com
Roney & Co. http://www.roney.com
Charles Schwab & Co., Inc. http://www.schwab.com
Net Trades: $29.95
Muriel Siebert & Co., Inc. http://www.msiebert.com
Net Trades: $25
Scott & Stringfellow http://www.scottstringfellow.com
Scottsdale Securities http://www.discountbroker.com
Net Trades: $9 ($10,000 min balance)
Smith Barney http://www.smithbarney.com
Southwest Securities http://www.swst.com
Sovereign Securities http://www.mydiscountbroker.com
Tucker Anthony http://www.tucker-anthony.com

Netwise Tidbit

Discount Brokers Ranked
http://www.astro.lsa.umich.edu/users/philf/www/discount.html
Rankings and information on a number of discount brokers.

Newsletters On The Internet

For investors who can't get enough of investment newsletters, the internet is the perfect place to shop. While many of the newsletters listed below are not free, most pay services offer free samples or free trial subscriptions. While you're browsing, remember that newsletters, like people, range in personality from conservative to outright radical. Make sure a particular newsletter has a risk and return strategy that you're comfortable with before using it to choose investments.

2 for 1 http://www.2-for-1.com
Monthly newsletter focusing on common stocks that have recently split.

A.S.K. Financial Digest http://www.askd.com
Monthly analysis of the stock and bond markets, plus the economy, for investors with a 1-12 month time horizon.

AAMES Daily Email Newsletter http://adnetsolfp2.adnetsol.com/aames
Daily e-mail letter highlights short-term stock trading suggestions.

Accelerating Grth. Stockselector http://www.dirs.com/invest/ags
Monthly selection of dynamic growth high tech companies with explosive stock price appreciation potential.

Alaska's Voice of the North http://www.ptialaska.net/~voice
Buy and sell signals from a proprietary database in the Great White North.

Alert-IPO! http://www.ostman.com/alert-ipo
Daily automated e-mail notification of IPO filings accompanied by detailed reports about the filing companies.

Astrologers Fund, Inc., The http://www.afund.com
Investing by the stars.

Aurex Market Masters http://www.aurex.com
Several levels of subscription services with features such as PowerPlay stocks that are likely to be short-term hits.

Bedford & Assoc. Rsch. Group http://www.baresearch.com
Intraday options reports, daily stock picks, the Cycle Watch Institutional Advisor

Berkshire Online http://www.growth.com
Free timely information about small, aggressive, growth companies.

Buttonwood Financial Resources http://www.buttonwood.net
Get free trials, and subscribe to a growing number of newsletters.

Cabot Market Letter http://www.cabotm.com
Advice from Carlton Lutts on fast-growing stocks of less well-known companies, published every other week.

CDA/Investnet's Insiders' Chron. http://www.cda.com/investnet
Devoted to insider trading data and analysis.

Cedar Group, The http://www.cdrgrp.com
Detailed weekly rankings and performance statistics on mutual funds.

Classic Asset Management http://www.moneymanagement.com
Monthly newsletter focusing on momentum investing.

Cognotick Market Service http://www.cognotick.com
Daily information on resistance and support price targets, oscillation changes and chart divergence.

Contrarian's View, The http://fennel.assumption.edu/view
Includes market outlook discussion and short-term buy and sell indicators based on NYSE advance/decline numbers.

Day Traders On-line http://www.daytraders.com
Timely market research for both short-term investing and intraday trading, delivered by e-mail, plus a short-term model portfolio.

Deemer's Market Strategies http://www.4w.com/deemer
Market comments and opinions for sophisticated institutional investors.

Doctor's Report http://www.cpas4docs.com
Monthly planning ideas and information for doctors.

Dogs of the Dow http://www.dogsofthedow.com
A newsletter for one of the lowest-maintenance investment strategies out there.

Early Warning Report http://www.subscriptions.com/beacon
Covers major U.S. and world political, economic and military events that affect investments.

F.X.C. Newsletter http://www.fxcinv.com
E-mailed twice monthly with in-depth research on recommended companies, plus direct personal investment advice available as part of your subscription.

Growth Stock Gazette, The http://home.navisoft.com/gsg
Concentrates on high growth and high return on stocks.

H&H Investment Forum http://www.hh-forum.com
Seeks out fundamentally sound NASDAQ stocks priced at or below $1.25, provides buy and sell prices, fundamental data on stocks, plus a bulletin board and real-time chat rooms.

Holt Stock Report http://metro.turnpike.net/holt
Daily e-mail and web report of new highs, lows and volume increases for stocks and optionable stocks.

Hussman Econometrics http://www.concentric.net/~hussman
Features econometric forecasts for the stock, bond, and precious metals markets from John P. Hussman Ph.D., a professor of economics and international finance at the University of Michigan.

Information Line http://www.intelweb.com/infopass.htm
Covers foreign exchange, precious metals and overseas banking.

Insider-Information http://www.netgate.net/~forecast
Weekly price forecasts via e-mail.

inSight inFormation http://avidinfo.com
Short-term stock and options trading.

Internet Financial Connection http://www.ifcstocks.com
This newsletter brings together stock picks and market commentary from a large number of other newsletters to present a single-source option for the information.

Investing.com http://www.investing.com
Free monthly investing news updates by e-mail.

Investment Reporter Magazine http://members.aol.com/investrptr
Information about undiscovered microcap companies not covered by the general media.

Investors Free Forum http://www.investorsforum.com
A great source for free investment offers such as sweepstakes, gift certificates and free trials.

Investors Newsletter Digest http://www.investorsnews.com
Opinions and recommendations of top financial strategists and newsletters, all gathered together in one place.

Investor's Nightly Journal http://www.libertyresearch.com
Nightly e-mail newsletter with investment ideas and trading signals on a hand-picked portfolio of stocks.

J. Patrick Calby Report http://www.2020tech.com/pcalby
Stock recommendations and suggestions by e-mail.

Jack's Picks http://www.jackm.com
Written with the novice investor in mind, this newsletter strives to explain concepts using plain language.

Jag Notes http://www.jagnotes.com
A concise daily overview of morning comments from the major Wall Street research firms.

JJJ's Buy Low Sell High Advisor http://www.jjjinvesting.com
Articles, model portfolios, and recommended stocks/closed-end funds, plus an investing book you can purchase in print or download for free.

Kostech SmallCap Research http://www.kostech.com
Searches for young companies with new and innovative products and services, whose stock is currently trading under $10 per share.

McMillan Analysis Corporation http://www.spidertel.com/mcmillan
Daily stocks selected by monitoring unusual option trading volume.

Money Talks http://www.talks.com
Free daily investment magazine for the serious individual investor.

NetPicks Investment System http://www.netpicks.holowww.com
Aggressive options trading recommendations.

Newsletter Access http://www.newsletteraccess.com
This online database of 5,000 newsletters includes profiles of more than 400 investment letters, including online forms to request additional information, trial copies, etc.

Newsletter Network http://www.margin.com
Visitors can obtain free sample copies, and subscribers can download their newsletters directly.

Olsen & Associates http://www.olsen.ch
Real-time directional forecasts, market timing information and model-driven buy/sell recommendations.

PASCO Research http://www.pasco-res.com
Register for 3 months of free Daily Reports from these cycle analysts who discover, monitor and report cycles relevant to equity investments.

Pinson's Digest & Hotline http://www.tfc.com/pinson
Features insider trading activity, Fidelity Sector mutual fund outlook, conservative and speculative growth stocks, no-load mutual funds, asset allocation tables, monitored stocks for current buy, sell, & hold recommendations and more.

The Pitbull Investor http://com.primenet.com/pitbull
Weekly newsletter provides trading recommendations based on the Pitbull system.

Pristine Day Trader, The http://www.wso.com
Daily stock recommendations for active traders.

The Privateer http://www.the-privateer.com
This Australian market letter covers the global financial and economic situation and tracks several portfolios of stocks on the Australian stock market.

Prudential Securities http://www.prusec.com
Eight daily market commentaries, plus Investment Strategy Weekly.

Regal Discount Securities http://www.regaldiscount.com
Regal's Rewarding Times covers a number of investment topics.

Rolling Stocks Report http://www.qasnet.com
Identifies stocks that are "rolling" (cycling between a particular high and low).

Security Traders Handbook http://www.prars.com
This monthly financial newspaper is distributed to Wall Street market makers, stock brokers, and individual investors.

Select Timing Service http://www.dollarlink.com
Short-term mutual fund switching system.

Sensible Investment Strategies http://www.seninvest.com
SIS will formulate a customized investment strategy based upon answers you provide to their proprietary questionnaire.

SGA Goldstar Research http://sgagoldstar.com/sga
Timely stock market research including their special Whisper Stock information.

Spencer Financial http://www.spencerletter.com
Monthly detailed updates and analysis of featured companies.

Stocknet Timing Report http://www.consulan.com/stocknet
Mutual fund timing alerts by e-mail.

Steward Analytics, Inc. http://members.aol.com/oexchaos
Daily research service for sophisticated options, equity, and mutual fund traders.

Stockplayer http://www.stockplayer.com
Profiles stocks offering substantial appreciation potential.

TFC Market Mavens Stock Rpt. http://www.tfc.com
Home of Wall Street's Market Mavens, plus information and free trials from a number of investment newsletters.

Timing is Everything http://www.ilinks.net/mktimer
Market timing system for improving long-term returns of mutual fund investments with a low portfolio risk.

Trend Analysis Ltd http://www.CityScape.co.uk/index
Daily commentary on foreign exchange, financial futures, metals and market indices from the United Kingdom.

Vanguard Group http://www.vanguard.com
Click on Request Literature and then Newsstand for several newsletters.

Walkrich Investment Advisors http://www.mo.net/walkrich
Weekly stock forecasts using a neural network computer model.

Wall Street News http://www.IMService.com/forecasts
Forecasts on trends, timing, sentiment, prices and turning points.

Westergaard Online http://www.westergaard.com
Featuring Sturza's Medical Investment Letter and The Daily Interpreter.

Wright Investors' Service http://www.wisi.com
Weekly investment commentary, advice and analysis.

Netwise Tidbit

Investools
http://investools.com

In the Newsletters section of this site, you can find information on more than 300 individual newsletters, in categories such as: Closed-end Funds, Commodities, IPOs, Precious Metals, and Insider Trading.

Offline—Things a Stock Broker Can Give You For Free

Free stuff isn't only available in cyberspace. A full-service stock broker should be happy to provide you with all of the information listed below. Even if you're not a client, many brokers will be willing to provide this kind of information to you in the hopes that you may become a client in the future. Discount brokers generally provide fewer benefits, but still may give away some of the information listed; you won't know unless you ask.

Many brokerage firms give away generic booklets on the following:

- zero-coupon bonds
- municipal bonds
- corporate bonds
- convertible bonds
- options
- preferred stock
- margin accounts
- gifts of securities to minors
- retirement planning

Brokers should also be willing to provide you with:

- internal research reports
- lists of top stock ideas
- Value Line reports
- Morningstar reports
- Standard & Poor's reports

Power Index

Premier Sites

Bank Rate Monitor	http://www.bankrate.com
Bloomberg Personal	http://www.bloomberg.com
DBC Online	http://www.dbc.com
Dorsey, Wright & Assoc.	http://www.dorseywright.com
Eanalytics	http://www.e-analytics.com
Holt Stock Report	http://metro.turnpike.net/holt/index.html
Infoseek	http://www.infoseek.com
Internal Revenue Service	http://www.irs.ustreas.gov/prod
Motley Fool, The	http://www.fool.com
NETworth	http://networth.galt.com
NYU EDGAR	http://edgar.stern.nyu.edu
Prudential Securities	http://www.prusec.com
Research Mag./InvestorNet	http://www.researchmag.com

12-Month Earnings

Chicago Tribune	http://www.webpoint.com/stocks/tribune
stockprofiles.com	http://www.stockprofiles.com

5-Year High & Low

Chicago Tribune	http://www.webpoint.com/stocks/tribune

52 Week High & Low

American Stock Exchange	http://www.amex.com
Chicago Tribune	http://www.webpoint.com/stocks/tribune
CNNfn	http://cnnfn.com
DBC Online	http://www.dbc.com
E*TRADE	http://www.etrade.com
Infoseek	http://www.infoseek.com
Lombard	http://www.lombard.com
My Yahoo!	http://my.yahoo.com
NETworth	http://networth.galt.com
Pathfinder	http://pathfinder.com
PC Financial Network	http://www.pcfn.com
PC Quote	http://www.pcquote.com
Quote.com	http://www.quote.com
Research Mag./InvestorNet	http://www.researchmag.com
Reuters MoneyNet.com	http://www.moneynet.com
Charles Schwab & Co., Inc.	http://www.schwab.com
stockprofiles.com	http://www.stockprofiles.com

Addresses of Companies

Corporate Financials Online	http://www.cfonews.com
My Yahoo!	http://my.yahoo.com
stockprofiles.com	http://www.stockprofiles.com

ADR (American Depositary Receipts) Information

DBC Online	http://www.dbc.com
Research Mag./InvestorNet	http://www.researchmag.com

Advance/Decline Numbers

Holt Stock Report	http://metro.turnpike.net/holt/index.html
PC Quote	http://www.pcquote.com
Reuters MoneyNet.com	http://www.moneynet.com

Annual Dividend

Chicago Tribune	http://www.webpoint.com/stocks/tribune
NETworth	http://networth.galt.com
stockprofiles.com	http://www.stockprofiles.com

Annual Report Dates by Company

stockprofiles.com	http://www.stockprofiles.com

Annual Yield

Chicago Tribune	http://www.webpoint.com/stocks/tribune

Answers to Questions (Free)

Eanalytics	http://www.e-analytics.com

Appreciation Ranking Lists

Eanalytics	http://www.e-analytics.com

Articles

AAII	http://www.aaii.org
American Stock Exchange	http://www.amex.com
Avid Info	http://avidinfo.com
Bank of America	http://www.bankamerica.com
Bank Rate Monitor	http://www.bankrate.com
Bloomberg Personal	http://www.bloomberg.com
CNNfn	http://cnnfn.com
DBC Online	http://www.dbc.com
DRP IRA	http://www.drpira.com
Eanalytics	http://www.e-analytics.com
Fidelity Investments	http://www.fid-inv.com
Individual Investor Services	http://www.investor.nasd.com
Motley Fool, The	http://www.fool.com
Pathfinder	http://pathfinder.com
PC Financial Network	http://www.pcfn.com
Prudential Securities	http://www.prusec.com
Regal Discount Securities	http://www.regaldiscount.com
Research Mag./InvestorNet	http://www.researchmag.com
T. Rowe Price	http://www.troweprice.com
Univ. of Missouri-St. Louis	http://anasazi.umsl.edu
Vanguard Group	http://www.vanguard.com

Asset Allocation

AAII	http://www.aaii.org
Bank of America	http://www.bankamerica.com
Vanguard Group	http://www.vanguard.com

Average Daily Volume

Lombard	http://www.lombard.com
stockprofiles.com	http://www.stockprofiles.com

Bank Rates

Bank Rate Monitor	http://www.bankrate.com
DBC Online	http://www.dbc.com

Banking

Bank of America	http://www.bankamerica.com
Bank Rate Monitor	http://www.bankrate.com

Banking - Internet Account Access

Bank of America	http://www.bankamerica.com

Beta

stockprofiles.com	http://www.stockprofiles.com

Biggest Gainer/Loser Lists

American Stock Exchange	http://www.amex.com
Bloomberg Personal	http://www.bloomberg.com
Chicago Tribune	http://www.webpoint.com/stocks/tribune
CNNfn	http://cnnfn.com
DBC Online	http://www.dbc.com
Infoseek	http://www.infoseek.com
PC Financial Network	http://www.pcfn.com
Quote.com	http://www.quote.com

Bond Data

Bloomberg Personal	http://www.bloomberg.com
CNNfn	http://cnnfn.com
DBC Online	http://www.dbc.com

Bond Information

AAII	http://www.aaii.org
Avid Info	http://avidinfo.com
Bank of America	http://www.bankamerica.com
Bloomberg Personal	http://www.bloomberg.com
CNNfn	http://cnnfn.com
DBC Online	http://www.dbc.com
Eanalytics	http://www.e-analytics.com
Prudential Securities	http://www.prusec.com
T. Rowe Price	http://www.troweprice.com

Bond Quotes

CNNfn	http://cnnfn.com
DBC Online	http://www.dbc.com
Eanalytics	http://www.e-analytics.com

Book Value

stockprofiles.com	http://www.stockprofiles.com

Brokers

Aufhauser / WealthWEB	http://www.aufhauser.com
E*TRADE	http://www.etrade.com
Fidelity Investments	http://www.fid-inv.com
Lombard	http://www.lombard.com
PC Financial Network	http://www.pcfn.com
Prudential Securities	http://www.prusec.com
Regal Discount Securities	http://www.regaldiscount.com
Charles Schwab & Co., Inc.	http://www.schwab.com
T. Rowe Price	http://www.troweprice.com

Brokers - Disclosure of Information

Individual Investor Services	http://www.investor.nasd.com

Brokers - Information

AAII	http://www.aaii.org
Individual Investor Services	http://www.investor.nasd.com
Prudential Securities	http://www.prusec.com
Stock Club	http://stockclub.com

Brokers - Internet Trading

Aufhauser / WealthWEB	http://www.aufhauser.com
E*TRADE	http://www.etrade.com
Lombard	http://www.lombard.com
PC Financial Network	http://www.pcfn.com
Charles Schwab & Co., Inc.	http://www.schwab.com

Calculators - Asset Allocation

Bank of America	http://www.bankamerica.com
Vanguard Group	http://www.vanguard.com

Calculators - Budget

Pathfinder	http://pathfinder.com

Calculators - Education Cost

Bloomberg Personal	http://www.bloomberg.com
Fidelity Investments	http://www.fid-inv.com
Individual Investor Services	http://www.investor.nasd.com

Calculators - Insurance

Lombard	http://www.lombard.com

Calculators - Investment Personality

Bank of America	http://www.bankamerica.com
Fidelity Investments	http://www.fid-inv.com
Prudential Securities	http://www.prusec.com
Vanguard Group	http://www.vanguard.com

Calculators - IRA Deductibility

Bank of America	http://www.bankamerica.com

Calculators - Loan

Individual Investor Services	http://www.investor.nasd.com
interactive nest egg	http://nestegg.iddis.com

Calculators - Mortgage

Bloomberg Personal	http://www.bloomberg.com
Pathfinder	http://pathfinder.com

Calculators - PEG/YPEG (Fool Ratio)

Motley Fool, The	http://www.fool.com

Calculators - Retirement

Bank of America	http://www.bankamerica.com
Fidelity Investments	http://www.fid-inv.com
Individual Investor Services	http://www.investor.nasd.com
interactive nest egg	http://nestegg.iddis.com
Pathfinder	http://pathfinder.com
Prudential Securities	http://www.prusec.com
T. Rowe Price	http://www.troweprice.com
Vanguard Group	http://www.vanguard.com

Calendars of Economic Reports

Briefing.Com	http://www.briefing.com
DBC Online	http://www.dbc.com
Eanalytics	http://www.e-analytics.com
interactive nest egg	http://nestegg.iddis.com

Canadian Exchanges - Quotes

NETworth	http://networth.galt.com

Cash Per Share

stockprofiles.com	http://www.stockprofiles.com

Charts

DBC Online	http://www.dbc.com
Dorsey, Wright & Assoc.	http://www.dorseywright.com
Individual Investor	http://www.iionline.com
Infoseek	http://www.infoseek.com
Lombard	http://www.lombard.com
My Yahoo!	http://my.yahoo.com
NASDAQ	http://www.nasdaq.com
NETworth	http://networth.galt.com
PC Financial Network	http://www.pcfn.com
PC Quote	http://www.pcquote.com
Quote.com	http://www.quote.com
Research Mag./InvestorNet	http://www.researchmag.com
Reuters MoneyNet.com	http://www.moneynet.com
Charles Schwab & Co., Inc.	http://www.schwab.com
Zacks	http://www.zacks.com

Charts - Comparative Percentage

NETworth	http://networth.galt.com
PC Financial Network	http://www.pcfn.com

Charts - Daily

DBC Online	http://www.dbc.com
Individual Investor	http://www.iionline.com
Infoseek	http://www.infoseek.com
Lombard	http://www.lombard.com
My Yahoo!	http://my.yahoo.com
NETworth	http://networth.galt.com
PC Financial Network	http://www.pcfn.com
PC Quote	http://www.pcquote.com
Quote.com	http://www.quote.com
Reuters MoneyNet.com	http://www.moneynet.com
Charles Schwab & Co., Inc.	http://www.schwab.com

Charts - Intraday

Lombard	http://www.lombard.com
NASDAQ	http://www.nasdaq.com
PC Financial Network	http://www.pcfn.com
Quote.com	http://www.quote.com
Charles Schwab & Co., Inc.	http://www.schwab.com

Charts - Monthly

Lombard	http://www.lombard.com

NASDAQ	http://www.nasdaq.com
PC Financial Network	http://www.pcfn.com
Quote.com	http://www.quote.com

Charts - Moving Average Lines

Infoseek	http://www.infoseek.com
NETworth	http://networth.galt.com
PC Financial Network	http://www.pcfn.com
PC Quote	http://www.pcquote.com
Reuters MoneyNet.com	http://www.moneynet.com

Charts - Point & Figure

Dorsey, Wright & Assoc.	http://www.dorseywright.com

Charts - Weekly

Infoseek	http://www.infoseek.com
Lombard	http://www.lombard.com
NETworth	http://networth.galt.com
PC Financial Network	http://www.pcfn.com
Quote.com	http://www.quote.com
Research Mag./InvestorNet	http://www.researchmag.com
Reuters MoneyNet.com	http://www.moneynet.com
Charles Schwab & Co., Inc.	http://www.schwab.com

Charts - Yearly

Lombard	http://www.lombard.com
NETworth	http://networth.galt.com

Chat Rooms

Avid Info	http://avidinfo.com

Commodities & Futures Information

CNNfn	http://cnnfn.com
Eanalytics	http://www.e-analytics.com

Company Profiles

Aufhauser / WealthWEB	http://www.aufhauser.com
Business Wire	http://www.businesswire.com
Individual Investor	http://www.iionline.com
Infoseek	http://www.infoseek.com
Motley Fool, The	http://www.fool.com
My Yahoo!	http://my.yahoo.com
Pathfinder	http://pathfinder.com
Research Mag./InvestorNet	http://www.researchmag.com
stockprofiles.com	http://www.stockprofiles.com
Zacks	http://www.zacks.com

Complaint Filing Information

Individual Investor Services	http://www.investor.nasd.com
NASDAQ	http://www.nasdaq.com

Consumer Loans

Bank Rate Monitor	http://www.bankrate.com

Contests/Games

Avid Info	http://avidinfo.com
E*TRADE	http://www.etrade.com
Fidelity Investments	http://www.fid-inv.com

Motley Fool, The http://www.fool.com

Credit Cards

Bank Rate Monitor http://www.bankrate.com

Currency - New Highs & Lows

Holt Stock Report http://metro.turnpike.net/holt/index.html

Currency Forecasts

Avid Info http://avidinfo.com
Bank of America http://www.bankamerica.com

Currency Quotes

Bloomberg Personal http://www.bloomberg.com
Chicago Tribune http://www.webpoint.com/stocks/tribune
CNNfn http://cnnfn.com
Eanalytics http://www.e-analytics.com
Holt Stock Report http://metro.turnpike.net/holt/index.html
Infoseek http://www.infoseek.com

Current Ratio

stockprofiles.com http://www.stockprofiles.com

Current Yield

American Stock Exchange http://www.amex.com
DBC Online http://www.dbc.com
PC Quote http://www.pcquote.com

Discussion Forums

Individual Investor http://www.iionline.com
Motley Fool, The http://www.fool.com
Stock Club http://stockclub.com

Discussion Forums By Stock

Individual Investor http://www.iionline.com
Motley Fool, The http://www.fool.com
Stock Club http://stockclub.com

Dividend Frequency

American Stock Exchange http://www.amex.com
PC Quote http://www.pcquote.com

Dividend Re-Investment Plans

AAII http://www.aaii.org
Direct Stock Purchase Plans http://www.netstockdirect.com/lists/ch.html
DRIP Guide http://www.cs.cmu.edu/~jdg/drip.html
DRP IRA http://www.drpira.com
No-Load Stocks Info http://noload.base.org

Dividend Yield

Lombard http://www.lombard.com
NETworth http://networth.galt.com
stockprofiles.com http://www.stockprofiles.com

Dividends Per Share

CNNfn http://cnnfn.com
DBC Online http://www.dbc.com
My Yahoo! http://my.yahoo.com
NETworth http://networth.galt.com

Earnings Surprises, Daily

Zacks	http://www.zacks.com

Economic Reports

Reuters MoneyNet.com	http://www.moneynet.com

Economic Forecasts

Bank of America	http://www.bankamerica.com

EDGAR Access

Business Wire	http://www.businesswire.com
My Yahoo!	http://my.yahoo.com
NASDAQ	http://www.nasdaq.com
NYU EDGAR	http://edgar.stern.nyu.edu
Pathfinder	http://pathfinder.com

EDGAR Information

NYU EDGAR	http://edgar.stern.nyu.edu

Estate Planning

AAII	http://www.aaii.org

Ex-Dividend Amounts

American Stock Exchange	http://www.amex.com
My Yahoo!	http://my.yahoo.com
NETworth	http://networth.galt.com

Ex-Dividend Dates

Lombard	http://www.lombard.com
DBC Online	http://www.dbc.com
NETworth	http://networth.galt.com
PC Quote	http://www.pcquote.com

Exchange Rates

Chicago Tribune	http://www.webpoint.com/stocks/tribune
CNNfn	http://cnnfn.com
Eanalytics	http://www.e-analytics.com
Infoseek	http://www.infoseek.com

Financial Planning

AAII	http://www.aaii.org
Eanalytics	http://www.e-analytics.com
Fidelity Investments	http://www.fid-inv.com
interactive nest egg	http://nestegg.iddis.com
Motley Fool, The	http://www.fool.com
Prudential Securities	http://www.prusec.com
Research Mag./InvestorNet	http://www.researchmag.com

Float

stockprofiles.com	http://www.stockprofiles.com

Free Books

Bank Rate Monitor	http://www.bankrate.com

Free Trials

Bank Rate Monitor	http://www.bankrate.com
Dorsey, Wright & Assoc.	http://www.dorseywright.com
Electric Library	http://www.elibrary.com
TenPlus	http://www.iistenplus.com

Fundamental Stock Information

American Stock Exchange	http://www.amex.com
Chicago Tribune	http://www.webpoint.com/stocks/tribune
DBC Online	http://www.dbc.com
Individual Investor	http://www.iionline.com
Infoseek	http://www.infoseek.com
NETworth	http://networth.galt.com
Pathfinder	http://pathfinder.com
PC Quote	http://www.pcquote.com
Quote.com	http://www.quote.com
Research Mag./InvestorNet	http://www.researchmag.com
stockprofiles.com	http://www.stockprofiles.com

Futures & Commodities Information

Bloomberg Personal	http://www.bloomberg.com
Eanalytics	http://www.e-analytics.com

Getting Started

AAII	http://www.aaii.org
Bank of America	http://www.bankamerica.com
Bank Rate Monitor	http://www.bankrate.com
Bloomberg Personal	http://www.bloomberg.com
DBC Online	http://www.dbc.com
DRIP Guide	http://www.cs.cmu.edu/~jdg/drip.html
Eanalytics	http://www.e-analytics.com
Fidelity Investments	http://www.fid-inv.com
Individual Investor Services	http://www.investor.nasd.com
interactive nest egg	http://nestegg.iddis.com
Motley Fool, The	http://www.fool.com
Pathfinder	http://pathfinder.com
PC Financial Network	http://www.pcfn.com
Prudential Securities	http://www.prusec.com
Quote.com	http://www.quote.com
Regal Discount Securities	http://www.regaldiscount.com
Research Mag./InvestorNet	http://www.researchmag.com
Stock Club	http://stockclub.com
T. Rowe Price	http://www.troweprice.com
Univ. of Missouri-St. Louis	http://anasazi.umsl.edu
Vanguard Group	http://www.vanguard.com

Global Investment & Economic Information

AAII	http://www.aaii.org
Avid Info	http://avidinfo.com
Bank of America	http://www.bankamerica.com
Bloomberg Personal	http://www.bloomberg.com
DBC Online	http://www.dbc.com
Research Mag./InvestorNet	http://www.researchmag.com
T. Rowe Price	http://www.troweprice.com

Glossaries

AAII	http://www.aaii.org
Bank Rate Monitor	http://www.bankrate.com
DBC Online	http://www.dbc.com

Eanalytics	http://www.e-analytics.com
Individual Investor Services	http://www.investor.nasd.com
Motley Fool, The	http://www.fool.com
NASDAQ	http://www.nasdaq.com
PC Financial Network	http://www.pcfn.com
Prudential Securities	http://www.prusec.com
Vanguard Group	http://www.vanguard.com

Glossaries - Mortgage Terms

Bank Rate Monitor	http://www.bankrate.com

Glossaries - Mutual Fund Terms

PC Financial Network	http://www.pcfn.com
Vanguard Group	http://www.vanguard.com

Gold Quotes

Holt Stock Report	http://metro.turnpike.net/holt/index.html

Government Reports Schedule

Briefing.Com	http://www.briefing.com
Eanalytics	http://www.e-analytics.com

Graphs (see also Charts)

DBC Onlinc	http://www.dbc.com
Dorsey, Wright & Assoc.	http://www.dorseywright.com
Individual Investor	http://www.iionline.com
Infoseek	http://www.infoseek.com
Lombard	http://www.lombard.com
My Yahoo!	http://my.yahoo.com
NASDAQ	http://www.nasdaq.com
NETworth	http://networth.galt.com
PC Financial Network	http://www.pcfn.com
PC Quote	http://www.pcquote.com
Quote.com	http://www.quote.com
Research Mag./InvestorNet	http://www.researchmag.com
Reuters MoneyNet.com	http://www.moneynet.com
Charles Schwab & Co., Inc.	http://www.schwab.com
Zacks	http://www.zacks.com

Greatest % Rise In Volume Lists

CNNfn	http://cnnfn.com
DBC Online	http://www.dbc.com
Holt Stock Report	http://metro.turnpike.net/holt/index.html
Infoseek	http://www.infoseek.com

High EPS Growth with New High/Low Lists

Holt Stock Report	http://metro.turnpike.net/holt/index.html

High EPS Growth & Greatest % Rise In Volume Lists

Holt Stock Report	http://metro.turnpike.net/holt/index.html

Home Equity

Bank Rate Monitor	http://www.bankrate.com

Insurance Information

Eanalytics	http://www.e-analytics.com
interactive nest egg	http://nestegg.iddis.com

Interest Rate Forecasts

Bank of America	http://www.bankamerica.com

Interest Rates

Bank of America	http://www.bankamerica.com
CNNfn	http://cnnfn.com
Holt Stock Report	http://metro.turnpike.net/holt/index.html

International Investment Information

AAII	http://www.aaii.org
Avid Info	http://avidinfo.com
Bloomberg Personal	http://www.bloomberg.com
DBC Online	http://www.dbc.com
NETworth	http://networth.galt.com
Research Mag./InvestorNet	http://www.researchmag.com
T. Rowe Price	http://www.troweprice.com

International Market Indicators

Bloomberg Personal	http://www.bloomberg.com
CNNfn	http://cnnfn.com
Infoseek	http://www.infoseek.com

Intraday Market Commentary

Briefing.Com	http://www.briefing.com
DBC Online	http://www.dbc.com

Investment Club Information

NAIC	http://www.better-investing.org
Research Mag./InvestorNet	http://www.researchmag.com

Investment Strategies

AAII	http://www.aaii.org
Avid Info	http://avidinfo.com
Bank of America	http://www.bankamerica.com
Eanalytics	http://www.e-analytics.com
Individual Investor	http://www.iionline.com
Motley Fool, The	http://www.fool.com
NAIC	http://www.better-investing.org
Prudential Securities	http://www.prusec.com
Regal Discount Securities	http://www.regaldiscount.com
T. Rowe Price	http://www.troweprice.com
Univ. of Missouri-St. Louis	http://anasazi.umsl.edu

Investor Relations Contacts

Corporate Financials Online	http://www.cfonews.com
NETworth	http://networth.galt.com
Research Mag./InvestorNet	http://www.researchmag.com

IPO Schedules

IPO Central	http://www.ipocentral.com

IRA Deductibility

Bank of America	http://www.bankamerica.com

IRA Information

Bank of America	http://www.bankamerica.com
DRP IRA	http://www.drpira.com
T. Rowe Price	http://www.troweprice.com

Last Week's High & Low

Chicago Tribune	http://www.webpoint.com/stocks/tribune

Links to Financial Sites

Lombard	http://www.lombard.com
NETworth	http://networth.galt.com

Loans & Credit

Bank Rate Monitor	http://www.bankrate.com

Market Analysis

Avid Info	http://avidinfo.com
Bank of America	http://www.bankamerica.com
Bloomberg Personal	http://www.bloomberg.com
DBC Online	http://www.dbc.com
Eanalytics	http://www.e-analytics.com
Motley Fool, The	http://www.fool.com
NETworth	http://networth.galt.com
T. Rowe Price	http://www.troweprice.com

Market Cap

Chicago Tribune	http://www.webpoint.com/stocks/tribune
Corporate Financials Online	http://www.cfonews.com
DBC Online	http://www.dbc.com
Individual Investor	http://www.iionline.com
stockprofiles.com	http://www.stockprofiles.com

Market Commentary

American Stock Exchange	http://www.amex.com
Bank of America	http://www.bankamerica.com
DBC Online	http://www.dbc.com
Motley Fool, The	http://www.fool.com
NETworth	http://networth.galt.com
Prudential Securities	http://www.prusec.com
T. Rowe Price	http://www.troweprice.com

Market Commentary - Intraday

Briefing.Com	http://www.briefing.com
DBC Online	http://www.dbc.com
Prudential Securities	http://www.prusec.com

Market Forecasts

Avid Info	http://avidinfo.com
Bank of America	http://www.bankamerica.com
NETworth	http://networth.galt.com

Market Indicators

American Stock Exchange	http://www.amex.com
Aufhauser / WealthWEB	http://www.aufhauser.com
Bloomberg Personal	http://www.bloomberg.com
Chicago Tribune	http://www.webpoint.com/stocks/tribune
CNNfn	http://cnnfn.com
Corporate Financials Online	http://www.cfonews.com
DBC Online	http://www.dbc.com
Eanalytics	http://www.e-analytics.com
Holt Stock Report	http://metro.turnpike.net/holt/index.html

My Yahoo! http://my.yahoo.com
Pathfinder http://pathfinder.com
PC Financial Network http://www.pcfn.com
PC Quote http://www.pcquote.com
Prudential Securities http://www.prusec.com
Quote.com http://www.quote.com

Market Indicators - Intraday Charts

Infoseek http://www.infoseek.com
PC Financial Network http://www.pcfn.com
Reuters MoneyNet.com http://www.moneynet.com

Market Simulations

E*TRADE http://www.etrade.com

Metastock-Compatible Information

Zacks http://www.zacks.com

Mortgages

Bank Rate Monitor http://www.bankrate.com
Bloomberg Personal http://www.bloomberg.com

Most Active Lists

American Stock Exchange http://www.amex.com
Bloomberg Personal http://www.bloomberg.com
Chicago Tribune http://www.webpoint.com/stocks/tribune
CNNfn http://cnnfn.com
Holt Stock Report http://metro.turnpike.net/holt/index.html
Infoseek http://www.infoseek.com
PC Financial Network http://www.pcfn.com
Quote.com http://www.quote.com

Municipal Bonds

Bloomberg Personal http://www.bloomberg.com

Mutual Fund Companies

Fidelity Investments http://www.fid-inv.com
NETworth http://networth.galt.com
Prudential Securities http://www.prusec.com
T. Rowe Price http://www.troweprice.com
Vanguard Group http://www.vanguard.com

Mutual Fund Holdings

NYU EDGAR http://edgar.stern.nyu.edu
Quote.com http://www.quote.com

Mutual Fund Information

AAII http://www.aaii.org
Bloomberg Personal http://www.bloomberg.com
Chicago Tribune http://www.webpoint.com/stocks/tribune
DBC Online http://www.dbc.com
Fidelity Investments http://www.fid-inv.com
interactive nest egg http://nestegg.iddis.com
NETworth http://networth.galt.com
NYU EDGAR http://edgar.stern.nyu.edu
Pathfinder http://pathfinder.com
PC Financial Network http://www.pcfn.com

PC Quote	http://www.pcquote.com
Quote.com	http://www.quote.com
Research Mag./InvestorNet	http://www.researchmag.com
Charles Schwab & Co., Inc.	http://www.schwab.com
T. Rowe Price	http://www.troweprice.com
Vanguard Group	http://www.vanguard.com

Mutual Fund News

Bloomberg Personal	http://www.bloomberg.com
Quote.com	http://www.quote.com

Mutual Fund Performance Leader Lists

interactive nest egg	http://nestegg.iddis.com
NETworth	http://networth.galt.com
Quote.com	http://www.quote.com
Research Mag./InvestorNet	http://www.researchmag.com
Charles Schwab & Co., Inc.	http://www.schwab.com

Mutual Fund Profiles

NETworth	http://networth.galt.com
Prudential Securities	http://www.prusec.com
Quote.com	http://www.quote.com
Research Mag./InvestorNet	http://www.researchmag.com
Charles Schwab & Co., Inc.	http://www.schwab.com
Vanguard Group	http://www.vanguard.com

Mutual Fund Searches

NETworth	http://networth.galt.com
PC Financial Network	http://www.pcfn.com
Quote.com	http://www.quote.com
Research Mag./InvestorNet	http://www.researchmag.com

Mutual Fund Strategies

Quote.com	http://www.quote.com

Mutual Funds - No Load Funds

NETworth	http://networth.galt.com

Net Income

Research Mag./InvestorNet	http://www.researchmag.com

Net Profit Margin

Research Mag./InvestorNet	http://www.researchmag.com

New 52 Week Highs & Lows Lists

Infoseek	http://www.infoseek.com

New High/Low Lists

CNNfn	http://cnnfn.com
Holt Stock Report	http://metro.turnpike.net/holt/index.html
Infoseek	http://www.infoseek.com
Quote.com	http://www.quote.com

News

Bloomberg Personal	http://www.bloomberg.com
Business Wire	http://www.businesswire.com
Chicago Tribune	http://www.webpoint.com/stocks/tribune
Corporate Financials Online	http://www.cfonews.com
DBC Online	http://www.dbc.com

Electric Library	http://www.elibrary.com
Individual Investor	http://www.iionline.com
Infoseek	http://www.infoseek.com
Motley Fool, The	http://www.fool.com
My Yahoo!	http://my.yahoo.com
NASDAQ	http://www.nasdaq.com
Pathfinder	http://pathfinder.com
PC Financial Network	http://www.pcfn.com
Quote.com	http://www.quote.com
Research Mag./InvestorNet	http://www.researchmag.com
Reuters MoneyNet.com	http://www.moneynet.com

News - Intraday

CNNfn	http://cnnfn.com
DBC Online	http://www.dbc.com
My Yahoo!	http://my.yahoo.com
PC Financial Network	http://www.pcfn.com

News - Personalized

Infoseek	http://www.infoseek.com
My Yahoo!	http://my.yahoo.com

News - Searchable

Electric Library	http://www.elibrary.com
PC Financial Network	http://www.pcfn.com
PC Quote	http://www.pcquote.com

News By Company

Business Wire	http://www.businesswire.com
Corporate Financials Online	http://www.cfonews.com
Individual Investor	http://www.iionline.com
Infoseek	http://www.infoseek.com
My Yahoo!	http://my.yahoo.com
NASDAQ	http://www.nasdaq.com
PC Quote	http://www.pcquote.com
PC Financial Network	http://www.pcfn.com
Quote.com	http://www.quote.com
Research Mag./InvestorNet	http://www.researchmag.com
Reuters MoneyNet.com	http://www.moneynet.com

News Feeds

DBC Online	http://www.dbc.com

Newsletters

American Stock Exchange	http://www.amex.com
Eanalytics	http://www.e-analytics.com
Internal Revenue Service	http://www.irs.ustreas.gov/prod
Prudential Securities	http://www.prusec.com
Regal Discount Securities	http://www.regaldiscount.com
Vanguard Group	http://www.vanguard.com

No-Load Mutual Funds

NETworth	http://networth.galt.com
PC Financial Network	http://www.pcfn.com

No-Load Stocks

AAII	http://www.aaii.org
Direct Stock Purchase Plans	http://www.netstockdirect.com/lists/ch.html
DRIP Guide	http://www.cs.cmu.edu/~jdg/drip.html
No-Load Stocks Info	http://noload.base.org

Number of Shares

American Stock Exchange	http://www.amex.com
DBC Online	http://www.dbc.com
PC Quote	http://www.pcquote.com
stockprofiles.com	http://www.stockprofiles.com

Offline Information

Bank Rate Monitor	http://www.bankrate.com
Direct Stock Purchase Plans	http://www.netstockdirect.com/lists/ch.html
DRIP Guide	http://www.cs.cmu.edu/~jdg/drip.html
Fidelity Investments	http://www.fid-inv.com
Lombard	http://www.lombard.com
Motley Fool, The	http://www.fool.com
Prudential Securities	http://www.prusec.com
Quote.com	http://www.quote.com
T. Rowe Price	http://www.troweprice.com
Vanguard Group	http://www.vanguard.com

Optionable Stocks - Most Active

Holt Stock Report	http://metro.turnpike.net/holt/index.html

Optionable Stocks with New Highs/Lows

Holt Stock Report	http://metro.turnpike.net/holt/index.html

Optionable Stocks with Volume Increases

Holt Stock Report	http://metro.turnpike.net/holt/index.html

Options - Most Active

American Stock Exchange	http://www.amex.com
DBC Online	http://www.dbc.com
PC Quote	http://www.pcquote.com

Options Information

American Stock Exchange	http://www.amex.com
DBC Online	http://www.dbc.com
Eanalytics	http://www.e-analytics.com
Lombard	http://www.lombard.com
PC Financial Network	http://www.pcfn.com
Quote.com	http://www.quote.com
TenPlus	http://www.iistenplus.com

Options Trading Ideas

Eanalytics	http://www.e-analytics.com
TenPlus	http://www.iistenplus.com

Orders - Types of

Eanalytics	http://www.e-analytics.com
Motley Fool, The	http://www.fool.com

Personal Finance

Bank of America	http://www.bankamerica.com
Bank Rate Monitor	http://www.bankrate.com

CNNfn http://cnnfn.com
Eanalytics http://www.e-analytics.com
Fidelity Investments http://www.fid-inv.com
interactive nest egg http://nestegg.iddis.com
Motley Fool, The http://www.fool.com
Research Mag./InvestorNet http://www.researchmag.com

Phone Numbers of Companies

Business Wire http://www.businesswire.com
Corporate Financials Online http://www.cfonews.com
Individual Investor http://www.iionline.com
My Yahoo! http://my.yahoo.com
Research Mag./InvestorNet http://www.researchmag.com
stockprofiles.com http://www.stockprofiles.com

Point & Figure Charting

Dorsey, Wright & Assoc. http://www.dorseywright.com

Portfolio Management Concepts

AAII http://www.aaii.org
Prudential Securities http://www.prusec.com

Portfolio Price Alarms By E-mail

Quote.com http://www.quote.com

Portfolio Updates By E-mail

Quote.com http://www.quote.com
Reuters MoneyNet.com http://www.moneynet.com
Zacks http://www.zacks.com

Portfolio/Watch List Tracking

DBC Online http://www.dbc.com
Individual Investor http://www.iionline.com
Infoseek http://www.infoseek.com
Mercury Mail Inc. http://www.merc.com
My Yahoo! http://my.yahoo.com
NETworth http://networth.galt.com
PC Financial Network http://www.pcfn.com
PC Quote http://www.pcquote.com
Quote.com http://www.quote.com
Research Mag./InvestorNet http://www.researchmag.com
Reuters MoneyNet.com http://www.moneynet.com
T. Rowe Price http://www.troweprice.com
Vanguard Group http://www.vanguard.com

Premier Sites

Bank Rate Monitor http://www.bankrate.com
Bloomberg Personal http://www.bloomberg.com
DBC Online http://www.dbc.com
Dorsey, Wright & Assoc. http://www.dorseywright.com
Eanalytics http://www.e-analytics.com
Holt Stock Report http://metro.turnpike.net/holt/index.html
Infoseek http://www.infoseek.com
Internal Revenue Service http://www.irs.ustreas.gov/prod
Motley Fool, The http://www.fool.com

NETworth	http://networth.galt.com
NYU EDGAR	http://edgar.stern.nyu.edu
Prudential Securities	http://www.prusec.com
Research Mag./InvestorNet	http://www.researchmag.com

Price/Book

stockprofiles.com	http://www.stockprofiles.com

P/E Ratio

American Stock Exchange	http://www.amex.com
Chicago Tribune	http://www.webpoint.com/stocks/tribune
CNNfn	http://cnnfn.com
DBC Online	http://www.dbc.com
E*TRADE	http://www.etrade.com
Individual Investor	http://www.iionline.com
Infoseek	http://www.infoseek.com
Lombard	http://www.lombard.com
My Yahoo!	http://my.yahoo.com
NETworth	http://networth.galt.com
Pathfinder	http://pathfinder.com
PC Financial Network	http://www.pcfn.com
PC Quote	http://www.pcquote.com
Quote.com	http://www.quote.com
Research Mag./InvestorNet	http://www.researchmag.com
Reuters MoneyNet.com	http://www.moneynet.com
Charles Schwab & Co., Inc.	http://www.schwab.com
stockprofiles.com	http://www.stockprofiles.com

Quicken-Compatible Information

Mercury Mail Inc.	http://www.merc.com
NETworth	http://networth.galt.com
Quote.com	http://www.quote.com
Research Mag./InvestorNet	http://www.researchmag.com
T. Rowe Price	http://www.troweprice.com
Zacks	http://www.zacks.com

Quotes

American Stock Exchange	http://www.amex.com
Avid Info	http://avidinfo.com
Briefing.Com	http://www.briefing.com
Chicago Tribune	http://www.webpoint.com/stocks/tribune
CNNfn	http://cnnfn.com
Corporate Financials Online	http://www.cfonews.com
DBC Online	http://www.dbc.com
E*TRADE	http://www.etrade.com
Individual Investor	http://www.iionline.com
Lombard	http://www.lombard.com
My Yahoo!	http://my.yahoo.com
NASDAQ	http://www.nasdaq.com
NETworth	http://networth.galt.com
Pathfinder	http://pathfinder.com
PC Financial Network	http://www.pcfn.com
PC Quote	http://www.pcquote.com

NASDAQ	http://www.nasdaq.com
Pathfinder	http://pathfinder.com
PC Financial Network	http://www.pcfn.com
PC Quote	http://www.pcquote.com
Quote.com	http://www.quote.com
Regal Discount Securities	http://www.regaldiscount.com
Research Mag./InvestorNet	http://www.researchmag.com
Reuters MoneyNet.com	http://www.moneynet.com
Charles Schwab & Co., Inc.	http://www.schwab.com

Quotes - Option Symbol

Lombard	http://www.lombard.com
Reuters MoneyNet.com	http://www.moneynet.com

Quotes - Size of Last Trade

American Stock Exchange	http://www.amex.com
Lombard	http://www.lombard.com

Quotes - Tickers

NETworth	http://networth.galt.com

Quotes - Volume

American Stock Exchange	http://www.amex.com
Chicago Tribune	http://www.webpoint.com/stocks/tribune
CNNfn	http://cnnfn.com
DBC Online	http://www.dbc.com
E*TRADE	http://www.etrade.com
Individual Investor	http://www.iionline.com
Infoseek	http://www.infoseek.com
Lombard	http://www.lombard.com
My Yahoo!	http://my.yahoo.com
NASDAQ	http://www.nasdaq.com
NETworth	http://networth.galt.com
Pathfinder	http://pathfinder.com
PC Financial Network	http://www.pcfn.com
PC Quote	http://www.pcquote.com
Quote.com	http://www.quote.com
Regal Discount Securities	http://www.regaldiscount.com
Research Mag./InvestorNet	http://www.researchmag.com
Reuters MoneyNet.com	http://www.moneynet.com
Charles Schwab & Co., Inc.	http://www.schwab.com

Ranking In Industry By Company

Zacks	http://www.zacks.com

Rates - Consumer Loans

Bank Rate Monitor	http://www.bankrate.com
DBC Online	http://www.dbc.com

Rates - Credit Cards

Bank Rate Monitor	http://www.bankrate.com
DBC Online	http://www.dbc.com

Rates - Home Equity

Bank Rate Monitor	http://www.bankrate.com
DBC Online	http://www.dbc.com

Rates - Mortgage

Bank Rate Monitor	http://www.bankrate.com
DBC Online	http://www.dbc.com

Rates - Savings

Bank Rate Monitor	http://www.bankrate.com
DBC Online	http://www.dbc.com

Resistance

Research Mag./InvestorNet	http://www.researchmag.com

Retirement Planning

AAII	http://www.aaii.org
Bank of America	http://www.bankamerica.com
Bank Rate Monitor	http://www.bankrate.com
Eanalytics	http://www.e-analytics.com
Fidelity Investments	http://www.fid-inv.com
interactive nest egg	http://nestegg.iddis.com
Prudential Securities	http://www.prusec.com
Research Mag./InvestorNet	http://www.researchmag.com
T. Rowe Price	http://www.troweprice.com
Vanguard Group	http://www.vanguard.com

Return on Assets

stockprofiles.com	http://www.stockprofiles.com

Return on Equity

stockprofiles.com	http://www.stockprofiles.com

Revenue

Research Mag./InvestorNet	http://www.researchmag.com

Risk Tolerance

Bank of America	http://www.bankamerica.com
Fidelity Investments	http://www.fid-inv.com
Prudential Securities	http://www.prusec.com
T. Rowe Price	http://www.troweprice.com
Vanguard Group	http://www.vanguard.com

Rumors

Biotech Rumor Mill, The	http://www.tradesmart.com/rumor
Motley Fool, The	http://www.fool.com
Stock Club	http://stockclub.com

Sales Per Share

Research Mag./InvestorNet	http://www.researchmag.com
stockprofiles.com	http://www.stockprofiles.com

Savings

Bank of America	http://www.bankamerica.com
Bank Rate Monitor	http://www.bankrate.com
Pathfinder	http://pathfinder.com

SEC Filings

Business Wire	http://www.businesswire.com
Corporate Financials Online	http://www.cfonews.com
DBC Online	http://www.dbc.com
Infoseek	http://www.infoseek.com

NYU EDGAR http://edgar.stern.nyu.edu

Sector Analysis

Briefing.Com http://www.briefing.com

Seminars (Free)

Prudential Securities http://www.prusec.com

Shares Outstanding

American Stock Exchange http://www.amex.com
DBC Online http://www.dbc.com
PC Quote http://www.pcquote.com
stockprofiles.com http://www.stockprofiles.com

Software Downloads

Eanalytics http://www.e-analytics.com
Motley Fool, The http://www.fool.com
PC Quote http://www.pcquote.com
Reuters MoneyNet.com http://www.moneynet.com

Software Reviews

Eanalytics http://www.e-analytics.com

Stock Predictions

Biotech Rumor Mill, The http://www.tradesmart.com/rumor
Bloomberg Personal http://www.bloomberg.com
Briefing.Com http://www.briefing.com
Corporate Financials Online http://www.cfonews.com
DBC Online http://www.dbc.com
Dorsey, Wright & Assoc. http://www.dorseywright.com
Eanalytics http://www.e-analytics.com
Individual Investor http://www.iionline.com
Motley Fool, The http://www.fool.com
NAIC http://www.better-investing.org
Regal Discount Securities http://www.regaldiscount.com
Research Mag./InvestorNet http://www.researchmag.com
Stock Club http://stockclub.com

Stock Ideas

Biotech Rumor Mill, The http://www.tradesmart.com/rumor
DBC Online http://www.dbc.com
Dorsey, Wright & Assoc. http://www.dorseywright.com
Eanalytics http://www.e-analytics.com
Individual Investor http://www.iionline.com
Research Mag./InvestorNet http://www.researchmag.com
Stock Club http://stockclub.com
TenPlus http://www.iistenplus.com
Zacks http://www.zacks.com

Stock Splits

Eanalytics http://www.e-analytics.com

Stocks - Searching by Technical Criteria

Research Mag./InvestorNet http://www.researchmag.com

Support

Research Mag./InvestorNet http://www.researchmag.com

Symbol Searches

Chicago Tribune	http://www.webpoint.com/stocks/tribune
CNNfn	http://cnnfn.com
DBC Online	http://www.dbc.com
E*TRADE	http://www.etrade.com
Infoseek	http://www.infoseek.com
Lombard	http://www.lombard.com
NETworth	http://networth.galt.com
Pathfinder	http://pathfinder.com
PC Quote	http://www.pcquote.com
Quote.com	http://www.quote.com
Regal Discount Securities	http://www.regaldiscount.com
Research Mag./InvestorNet	http://www.researchmag.com
stockprofiles.com	http://www.stockprofiles.com

Tax Advice (Free)

Internal Revenue Service	http://www.irs.ustreas.gov/prod

Tax Code (Federal)

Internal Revenue Service	http://www.irs.ustreas.gov/prod
Taxing Times	http://www.scubed.com/tax/index.html

Tax Forms

interactive nest egg	http://nestegg.iddis.com
Internal Revenue Service	http://www.irs.ustreas.gov/prod
Taxing Times	http://www.scubed.com/tax/index.html

Tax Information

interactive nest egg	http://nestegg.iddis.com
Internal Revenue Service	http://www.irs.ustreas.gov/prod
Taxing Times	http://www.scubed.com/tax/index.html
T. Rowe Price	http://www.troweprice.com

Technical Analysis Information

Dorsey, Wright & Assoc.	http://www.dorseywright.com
Eanalytics	http://www.e-analytics.com

Technical Evaluations / Predictions by Stock

Research Mag./InvestorNet	http://www.researchmag.com

Technical Screening Tools

Research Mag./InvestorNet	http://www.researchmag.com

Total Debt/Equity

stockprofiles.com	http://www.stockprofiles.com

Volatility

American Stock Exchange	http://www.amex.com
DBC Online	http://www.dbc.com
PC Quote	http://www.pcquote.com

Volume Alert Lists

CNNfn	http://cnnfn.com
Holt Stock Report	http://metro.turnpike.net/holt/index.html
Quote.com	http://www.quote.com

Wall Street Analysis of Stocks

Research Mag./InvestorNet	http://www.researchmag.com

Zacks	http://www.zacks.com

Watch List/Portfolio Tracking

DBC Online	http://www.dbc.com
Individual Investor	http://www.iionline.com
Infoseek	http://www.infoseek.com
My Yahoo!	http://my.yahoo.com
NETworth	http://networth.galt.com
PC Financial Network	http://www.pcfn.com
PC Quote	http://www.pcquote.com
Quote.com	http://www.quote.com
Research Mag./InvestorNet	http://www.researchmag.com
Reuters MoneyNet.com	http://www.moneynet.com
T. Rowe Price	http://www.troweprice.com
Vanguard Group	http://www.vanguard.com

Web Locations of Companies

American Stock Exchange	http://www.amex.com
Infoseek	http://www.infoseek.com
My Yahoo!	http://my.yahoo.com

Worksheets - Asset Allocation

Bank of America	http://www.bankamerica.com

Worksheets - Cash Flow

Eanalytics	http://www.e-analytics.com

Worksheets - Life Insurance

Eanalytics	http://www.e-analytics.com

Worksheets - Net Worth

Eanalytics	http://www.e-analytics.com

Worksheets - Retirement Needs

Eanalytics	http://www.e-analytics.com
Research Mag./InvestorNet	http://www.researchmag.com

Yield

American Stock Exchange	http://www.amex.com
DBC Online	http://www.dbc.com
My Yahoo!	http://my.yahoo.com
PC Financial Network	http://www.pcfn.com
PC Quote	http://www.pcquote.com

Web Site Summaries

American Association of Individual Investors

http://www.aaii.org

Power Index Categories	
Articles	Glossaries
Asset Allocation	International Investment Information
Bond Information	Investment Strategies
Brokers - Information	Mutual Fund Information
Dividend Re-Investment Plans	No-Load Stocks
Estate Planning	Portfolio Management Concepts
Financial Planning	Retirement Planning
Getting Started	
Global Investment & Economic Information	

AAII "provides educational material to help individuals become better managers of their money."

Investing Basics

Start with How to Implement Your Strategy If You Are Starting From Scratch. Next take a look at Straightforward Answers to Common Questions on Retirement Plan Rules.

Financial Planning

Articles here include:

- The Life Cycle of Insurance Needs: A 30-Something Example
- Avoiding Multi-State Death Taxes: Steps to Establishing Your Domicile
- How Should You Hold Your Property?

Portfolio Management

These articles include:

- Living off Retirement Savings in a World of Uncertain Return Patterns
- Keeping Your Portfolio in Balance During Your Retirement Years
- Rebalancing your portfolio during your retirement years

Broker Issues

This section is all about finding and dealing with brokers. Issues covered include:

- Underwriters and Analyst Recommendations
- DRP Newsletters and Stock Purchasing Services

Mutual Funds

Articles include interviews with mutual fund industry professionals and topics such as A New Route Overseas: Country Indexing With WEBS & CountryBaskets.

Stocks

These articles present stock analysis techniques and investment strategies to help you pick stocks on your own. Articles include:

- Screening for Growth and Value Based on "What Works on Wall Street"
- The Bear Look
- Data Sources: Where to Find the Information That Meets Your Needs

Fixed Income

Articles here include:

- Timing and Selection Within the Bond Market: A Look at the Record
- A Top-Down Approach to Investing in the Municipal Bond Markets

Other Investments

Articles include:

- Index Stocks: An Introduction to SPDRs—S&P 500 Depositary Receipts
- Selecting the Mortgage Term: How to Compare the Alternative
- Indexed Annuities: Too High a Price for Market 'Protection'

American Stock Exchange

http://www.amex.com

Power Index Categories	
52 Week High & Low	Options - Most Active
Articles	Options Information
Biggest Gainer/Loser Lists	P/E Ratio
Current Yield	Quotes
Dividend Frequency	Quotes - Bid & Ask
Earnings Per Share	Quotes - Bid & Ask Size
Ex-Dividend Amounts	Quotes - Day's High & Low
Fundamental Stock Information	Quotes - Size of Last Trade
Market Commentary	Quotes - Volume
Market Indicators	Shares Outstanding
Most Active Lists	Volatility
Newsletters	Web Locations of Companies
Number of Shares	Yield

This is the American Stock Exchange's official web site. Since it only provides information on stocks listed at its own exchange, you may find it a bit limiting. The site does offer a good deal of information on its options and derivatives, and some general discussions on how the exchange works and how its operations differ from those of the other exchanges.

Market Summary

This is an end-of-day summary posted approximately 2 hours after market close each trading day. They'll tell you where the AMEX Index closed, and the total volume of shares traded on the exchange. For AMEX stocks, you can access lists of:

- Today's Most Active
- Today's Largest Percentage Gainers
- Today's Largest Percentage Decliners

If you follow the Options market, you can access:

- Today's Volume and Dollar Volume
- Advancers and Decliners
- Most Active Series
- Most Active Classes
- Most Active Series - One per Class

News

This is limited to news about the AMEX itself, such as word that a certain company has chosen to be listed on the exchange (as opposed to NYSE or NASDAQ). The area therefore has limited value to individual investors.

Listed Companies

All of the AMEX companies are listed alphabetically in 3 ways: by stock symbol; by company name; and by company web site (for those companies that have a homepage on the web).

By Stock Symbol & By Company Name These include all of the AMEX stocks. They're long lists, so it might take a minute or so to bring up if you have a slower modem. Clicking on a company's name will link you to a screen provided by PC Quote with Price and Fundamental data. Price Data includes:

- Last Sale
- Net Change
- Time of Last Sale
- Size of Last Sale
- Bid
- Ask
- Size of Bid & Ask
- Open
- High
- Low
- Volume
- Previous Close

Fundamental Data includes:

- 52 Week High & Low
- Volatility
- Ex-Dividend Amount
- Dividend Frequency
- Earnings per Share
- P/E Ratio
- Yield
- Shares Outstanding

By Homepages This lists only those companies who have their own sites on the web, with links to the web sites.

Options and Derivatives

Unfortunately, the Introduction to Derivative Securities still seems a little advanced, so if these concepts are new to you, you may have to look elsewhere.

There is, however, information on the AMEX's "Index Options Family":

- International Indexes (such as the Japan Index and the Mexico Index)
- Broad-Based Indexes (such as the S&P MidCap 400 Index and the Morgan Stanley Consumer Index)
- Sector Indexes (such as the Networking Index, the Airline Index and the Computer Technology Index)

You can also see complete lists of equity options sorted by stock symbol or company name. These lists provide you with the options symbol for the stock, but not any additional information.

Capital Markets This area contains information on:

- International Index Warrants
- Domestic Index Warrants
- Currency Warrants
- Index-Linked Notes
- Equity-Linked Notes
- other structured products

Information Exchange

Here AMEX is trying to go interactive (sort of). The idea is that various authors post articles in this section. You read the articles, e-mail your questions or comments directly to the author, and they follow up by posting selected Questions & Answers. You can find various discussions of the markets, such as an article entitled, "Capital Formation - How Companies Raise Money in the '90s," which discusses the current IPO market.

AMEX also posts transcripts of conference calls held by newsmakers in business, government and finance for the benefit of journalists.

There is also a link to the AMEXfacts newsletter. Each issue highlights a single topic, such as "Top 50 AMEX Stocks Held by Institutional Investors." These types of articles can be useful to an individual investor since they help view the market from a different perspective.

Netwise Tidbit

The New York Stock Exchange
http://www.nyse.com

Little valuable information, but cheaper than a trip to NYC to see the real thing.

Aufhauser/WealthWEB

http://www.aufhauser.com

Power Index Categories	
Brokers	Company Profiles
Brokers - Internet Trading	Market Indicators

This site will provide you with a detailed report on one company per day, but the catch is that you don't get to choose which company. Therefore, this is a good place to look for ideas for possible stocks to buy, but it won't do you any good if you've already chosen a company to research. The research report will provide you with most of the information you'll need to evaluate the potential of each company. Aufhauser charges $22.50 for internet trades of up to 399 shares.

Market Indices

The homepage will give you 10-minute delayed numbers for the Dow Jones and S&P 500 indices. They provide the current level, and the change from the previous trading day's closing figure. Each quote is date and time-stamped.

Free Research Report

A different company is profiled each trading day. To see the report, you'll have to provide your name, street address and e-mail address. This is not a stock recommendation, but each report does provide in-depth information on the chosen company. Information on the stock includes: Beta; average daily and monthly volume; annual dividend rate; and P/E ratio.

The next section of the report provides a comparison of the company's numbers to relevant industry groups and the applicable major market index (such as the S&P 500). This will compare net profit margin, return on equity, interest coverage, P/E ratio, dividend yield, price to tangible book, price to book, price to free cash flow, current ratio, LT Debt to Equity, total debt to equity, and growth statistics.

The Equity section will give you a history of the stock, including dates of the issuance and any stock splits, as well as the percentage of insider ownership.

The Historical Quarterly Results section will give you information by quarter for the past 4 years on Revenue and Earnings Per Share.

You'll also find sections on: Select Income Statement Items; Selected Balance Sheet Items; and Selected Statement of Cash Flow Items.

Avid Info

http://avidinfo.com

Power Index Categories	
Articles	International Investment Information
Bond Information	Investment Strategies
Chat Rooms	Market Analysis
Contests/Games	Market Forecasts
Currency Forecasts	Quotes
Global Investment & Economic Information	

This site is mostly an infomercial to get you to buy stuff, but it's worth visiting for its weekly stock game and for its web-based chat room.

Avid and its publications inSight inFormation and Mutual Momentum use technical analysis to predict market movement. They recommend aggressive trades with short-term holding periods. As noted, this site is mostly a pitch to get you to subscribe to the publication. For example, if you follow the link Specific Trade Recommendations, you get a description of the publication rather than any actual recommendations. However, they will explain their trading strategy to you if you're willing to sort through some infomercial-type pitches.

US Equities

To get to this section from the homepage, click on Daily *Heads-Up*. This page is updated daily, with a short description of the previous day's market indicators and predictions on what will happen today. For a similarly short recap of what's going on in the Bond market, take a look at Debt Instruments. There are also similar sections on Currencies & Precious Metals and World Markets. These aren't much more detailed than what you'd expect in a brief market recap on television.

Contest

They have a contest every week. The prize is one of their publications or tapes. Your mission: choose the stock that's going to see the biggest move (up or down) during the 1-week contest period.

Momentum Moments

This is one of the publications they're trying to sell you, dealing with mutual funds. Although it will be tough to find up-to-the-minute information, you will be able to peruse a few issues from the recent past. The issues include trading recommendations based on mutual fund portfolios tracked by the publication.

Traders Chat

This section is free but requires registration. You must provide your name, e-mail address, street address and phone number. You also choose an On-Screen Handle to use during the chat sessions. Once you arrive on the chat page, you can scroll down the discussions of the day and see what topics and rumors are hot, and what's not. Go to the bottom of the page to find a simple message box for you to post your own message to the page. Remember that anyone can post a message to these pages, and you should therefore take everything you hear with a grain of salt.

Second Opinion™

This section presents independent opinions from around the web on the following topics: stocks, bonds, metals, currencies, crude and world markets.

Quotes

Quotes are provided by DBC Online (also reviewed in this book). Symbol search is available, and with every quote you'll receive:

- Last price
- Change in price
- Previous price
- Low and High for the day
- Bid
- Ask
- Volume

Netwise Tidbit

Stocks.com
http://stocks.com

This site provides links to a number of financial web sites, dividing them by general categories such as Bonds and Brokers.

Bank of America

http://www.bankamerica.com

Power Index Categories	
Articles	Interest Rate Forecasts
Asset Allocation	Interest Rates
Banking	Investment Strategies
Banking - Internet Account Access	IRA Deductibility
Bond Information	IRA Information
Calculators - Asset Allocation	Market Analysis
Calculators - Investment Personality	Market Commentary
Calculators - IRA Deductibility	Market Forecasts
Calculators - Retirement	Personal Finance
Currency Forecasts	Retirement Planning
Economic Forecasts	Risk Tolerance
Getting Started	Savings
Global Investment & Economic Information	Worksheets - Asset Allocation

Since this site belongs to a bank, most of the information leans toward banking issues. Of special interest are the Investment Tools that can help you think about your savings plan and how to allocate your investment portfolio so that it matches your investment philosophy (if you didn't know you had an investment philosophy, maybe it's time to take a closer look at it!). The Money Tip of the Day will increase your knowledge of basic investment and financial issues.

Tools

Want a million dollars? Well, tell BofA how old you are and when you want to retire, and they'll tell you how much money you need to save every year to have that megabuck waiting for you on retirement day along with that gold watch (does anybody really hand out those gold watches anymore?). Click on the Tools menu, or follow the Spare Change link from the homepage. Since they're a bank, they'll assume a conservative return on investment over the years (such as 5.5%).

And, of course, they have some ideas on how you might start saving. First, check out BofA's asset allocation tool. It allows you to fill out a Personal Investment Profile, which is similar to the questionnaire you'll get if you open a brokerage account. These questions will force you to think about how you feel about your investments, and how much risk you're willing to take. The profile is anonymous; you won't be asked to identify yourself. When you submit your answers, BofA will tell you "What Your Answers Say About You," including suggestions on the composition of a Model Portfolio based on your answers. You then have the option of filling out a Worksheet to get BofA's opinion on whether your current investments match your profile. For example, your worksheet results may tell you that you are keeping too much money in short-term investments (such as savings accounts) and not enough money in fixed-income investments (such as bonds).

BofA also offers an IRA Deductibility Tool. Fill out a form indicating your tax filing status (such as Single), your total adjusted gross income, and whether or not you or your spouse participate in an employer-sponsored retirement plan, and BofA will tell you how large an IRA contribution can be deducted from your earned income. This tool is also anonymous.

What's New & Money Tip of The Day

Stop in here for a short and easily understood explanation of a financial topic, such as Preferred Stock.

Economics

This section has economic and financial reports, as well as investment recommendations by market sector (not by individual stocks, though).

The U.S. Economy BofA provides a thorough Weekly U.S. Economic Briefing. There is also a Monthly Survey of Wall Street Economists, providing a long term forecast for the economy including consensus estimates, with additional discussion on a single topic each month. There are also Economic Indicators such as Payroll Employment, and Special Reports such as "Economic outlook for major U.S. industries."

The Global Economy BofA provides a Weekly International Economic Briefing with market updates, upcoming data and events, upcoming U.S. economic indicators (with a chart including Market Expectation figures), and also figures on Germany, the United Kingdom, France, Japan, Australia, and Canada. There is a chart of interest rate and currency forecasts for the next 1, 3 and 6 months. The weekly briefing contains a great deal of technical information that will not be easy for beginners to digest.

Foreign Exchange Markets Technical Analyses are posted bi-weekly on how the U.S. Dollar is doing against the Yen, the Mark and the Pound.

Investment Strategies An Investment Overview & Strategy is posted here monthly. The Strategy portion includes asset allocation guidelines dependent on your overall investment objective. For example, if an investor's goal is "Growth," they might recommend allocating 75% of her portfolio to stocks, 25% to bonds, and none to cash. A separate section deals specifically with Equity Investment Strategy; here they discuss general factors and recommend buying stocks in particular market sectors (such as Technology), but no specific stocks are discussed. Other sections deal with:

- Fixed-Income Investment Strategy
- Tax-Exempt Bond Strategy
- Taxable Bond Strategy
- International Investment Strategy

There are also Forecasts & Consensus figures on:

- 3-month T-Bills
- 30-Year T-Bonds
- Real GDP Growth
- Inflation

Home Banking

BofA offers home banking, including access on the Internet. They'll be happy to explain the details to you in this section.

Netwise Tidbit

QuickQuote Insurance Agency
http://www.quickquote.com
Free, instant, on-line comparisons of more than 1,500 term life insurance policies and annuity plans.

Bank Rate Monitor

http://www.bankrate.com

Power Index Categories	
Premier Site	Loans & Credit
Articles	Mortgages
Bank Rates	Offline Information
Banking	Personal Finance
Consumer Loans	Rates - Consumer Loans
Credit Cards	Rates - Credit Cards
Free Books	Rates - Home Equity
Free Trials	Rates - Mortgage
Getting Started	Rates - Savings
Glossaries	Retirement Planning
Glossaries - Mortgage Terms	Savings
Home Equity	

If you give less of your money away, you'll have more to invest. Most investment guides will tell you that the first order of business in investing is getting your personal finances in order. This site can help you reshape your finances so that you're paying less for loans, and so that banks are paying you more for your money. Bank Rate Monitor sells 4 publications, but in the tradition of the web, they've lowered the volume on the sales pitch and given first priority to information that you can use.

Credit Cards

"Cut your credit card debt." This is the #1 piece of advice for new investors from just about everyone, so if you're carrying a balance on your plastic, take the time to read the advice in this section. They'll also tell you about the Best Credit Card Deals, for people who pay off their balances every month and for people who don't, with information on rates, fees and grace periods offered by each company.

BRM provides credit card rates by city if you want to buy your plastic locally. There's a separate section with rate information on Gold credit cards, and an explanation of Who qualifies for a gold card. There are also rates for secured credit cards, and an explanation of how you can build your credit history using them.

If you're not sure where to start, check out Choosing the right credit card.

Bank Rate Monitor's Credit Card section can help you get your credit card balance under control.

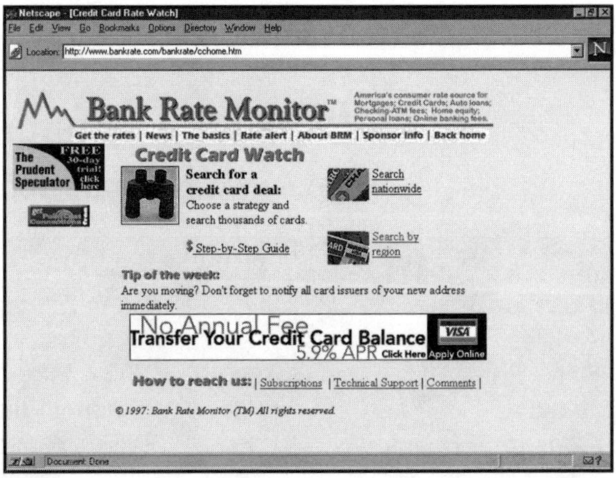

Mortgages

Mortgage Rates By City For most of the metropolitan areas in the U.S., you'll get the names and phone numbers of the largest-asset institutions, and the rates they're currently charging for 15-year and 30-year fixed rate loans, and 1-year adjustable-rate mortgages (ARMs). They'll also tell you how many Points are being charged for each type of mortgage.

Definitions of Mortgage Terms This will help you learn mortgage-speak.

Weekly Updates A new article is posted every week discussing the current state of the mortgage market. Past articles are also available. In addition, there are a number of articles on general topics, such as:

- Early mortgage payoff may pay off for you
- Why buydown mortgages are so popular
- How to protect your right to equal treatment

Savings

Nationwide and local deposit rates, by individual bank, for:

- money market accounts
- 6-month CDs
- 1-year CDs
- 2 ½-year CDs
- 5-year CDs

They'll also tell you how to open an account with an out-of-state bank. There are weekly articles on deposit rates, as well as tips on general issues like:

- How to calculate compound interest

- Understanding FDIC insurance on deposits
- Opening an insured revocable trust

Home Equity

A home equity line of credit combines a second mortgage with the features of a credit card (but hopefully with a lower interest rate). Rates for home equity lines of credit are provided by city. There's also advice on how to shop for a home equity line of credit, and the "Prime for life" interest rate feature.

Consumer Loans

Loans are rated by city. For each bank, you get the phone number plus current rates on New Car loans and Personal Loans. If you need a loan, it can be well worth your while to comparison shop. At any given time, the rates being charged by a metropolitan area's banks for personal loans can vary by 2.15% or more. You can also read about getting a loan from your stock broker instead of your banker.

Banking Tips

Here you'll find all of the site's tip-oriented articles gathered in one place, covering:

- retirement planning
- mortgages
- deposits
- loans
- credit cards
- ATM fees
- debit cards

Free Publication

If you're willing to take 5 minutes to complete a survey for them, BRM will send you one of the following for free: a 4-week subscription to the publication "100 Highest Yields"; the publication "Finding the best credit card deals"; or the publication "Finding the best mortgage deal."

The Biotech Rumor Mill

http://www.tradesmart.com/rumor

Power Index Categories	
Rumors	Stock Ideas
Stock Predictions	

Sometimes there is truth in advertising. This site offers exactly what the name says: biotech rumors (organized very nicely). The internet has basically created the world's biggest rumor mill (which is certainly no more reliable than any other rumor mill). Jump in, have fun, and don't take anything at face value.

Netwise Tidbit

invest-o-rama!

http://www.investorama.com

More than 4,300 links for investors, separated into around 60 categories.

Bloomberg Personal

http://www.bloomberg.com

Power Index Categories	
Premier Site	International Investment Information
Articles	International Market Indicators
Biggest Gainer/Loser Lists	Market Analysis
Bond Data	Market Indicators
Bond Information	Mortgages
Calculators - Education Cost	Most Active Lists
Calculators - Mortgage	Municipal Bonds
Currency Quotes	Mutual Fund Information
Futures & Commodities Information	Mutual Fund News
Getting Started	News
Global Investment & Economic Information	Quotes - Currency
	Stock Predictions

Bloomberg is in the information business, so the amount of information on this site can be overwhelming. If you want to get in and out quickly, just check out the top news stories and the stock columns. Follow the link Bloomberg News and then Bloomberg Columns to find Taking Stock, Poised to Rise and Poised to Fall.

Top News Story

Whenever you visit the site, the current top business story is right on the homepage for easy access.

Bloomberg News

Top financial headlines are listed on the first page of this section. Look in Top Business/Financial News for the full text of each story. U.S. Equity Preview highlights companies currently in the news. U.S. Equity Movers gives you the stories behind stocks that have just risen or fallen. To see summaries of the headline stories from papers in the U.S. and abroad, follow the Major Newspaper Headlines link. Mutual Fund News is just that; stories range from top-performing fund strategies to "Baby Boomers Start Saving for Retirement."

Found under Bloomberg Columns, Taking Stock is a weekly column on various aspects of the market, and it's a great place to learn. Check out Poised to Rise and Poised to Fall for predictions on which stocks will move next (remember to check the date of each individual article.

Financial Analysis

Bloomberg's Mortgage Calculator lets you enter the Loan Amount, Years, Payment Periods per year and Interest Rate, and the calculator will tell you what your monthly payments will be. Use of the tool is anonymous.

If you have or want kids and you're really brave (and you'd better be if you want kids), try out the Expected Future Education Cost Calculator to find out how much you should be putting away every month. This tool is extremely useful but not for the faint of heart.

World Markets

The main page of this section has a quick view of major market indexes:

- Dow Jones Industrial Average
- FT-SE 100 Index
- DAX Index
- NIKKEI 225 Index
- the Hang Seng Stock Index

There are also links to the following subsections.

World Equities Here you'll find the value, net change, and percentage change figures for major market indexes from: North/Latin America; Europe/Africa; and Asia/Pacific.

U.S. Treasuries This page provides you with information on the yields of U.S. Treasuries on a daily basis. There is also a graphic chart that helps compare the yields of each Treasury instrument.

Foreign Exchange This section provides world currency values. In other words, it compares international currencies with each other rather than with the U.S. Dollar. If you've ever wondered how the Turkmenistan Manat is doing against the Zimbabwe Dollar, here's your chance to find out.

Muni Bond Yields This area provides current and historical information on Triple-A Rated, Tax Exempt Insured Revenue Municipal Bonds.

Active Futures Contracts Bloomberg provides the following information on futures contracts:

- Time
- Current
- Change
- Open
- High
- Low
- Previous price

International Yield Curves This will give you the prices and yields for the international equivalents to U.S. Treasuries, from the governments of: Canada; France; Germany; Italy; Japan; the Netherlands; the United Kingdom; and, of course, the United States.

U.S. Index Movers This will give you quotes on the 5 or 6 member stocks that are currently moving the Dow or the S&P 500. They'll tell you how much each stock has moved, and how many points each index moved as a result.

U.S. Most Active Up/Down Bloomberg gives you the 6 stocks that were: Most Active by Volume; the biggest Gainers by Price Percentage; and the biggest Losers by Price Percentage.

Netwise Tidbit

Women's Wire
http://www.women.com/cash
Information for women on saving, investing, spending and life stages.

Briefing.Com

http://www.briefing.com

Power Index Categories	
Calendars of Economic Reports	Quotes
Government Reports Schedule	Sector Analysis
Intraday Market Commentary	Stock Ideas
Market Commentary - Intraday	

Go directly to the Introductory Service area by clicking on Always Free. If you're looking for stock ideas, make sure you visit Today's Selected Stock.

Market Comment

Updated constantly during the trading day, this will tell you where the market is heading and which economic factors are moving the market. In the Stock Ticker area, they highlight any stocks in the news or experiencing sharp moves.

Story Stocks

Updated continually during trading days, this will give you a quick glance at the dozen or so stocks that are making news. Each stock story is time-stamped.

Today's Selected Stock

This area provides an in-depth examination of a single company. Additional stock ideas can be found under Selected Stocks.

Market Calendar

Briefing provides the date and time of upcoming releases of economic data, as well as information on data that has just been released. For each, you'll get the forecast, the numbers the Market is expecting, and the previous numbers. They also provide a calendar of upcoming meetings and speeches that may move the markets.

Quotes

Real-time quotes on the market indexes can be found under Fast Check! Quotes and Portfolios will provide you with just that, supplied by Quote.com.

Sector Ratings

Here Briefing provides ratings and comments on the various market sectors, and on certain individual stocks as well. Click on Stock Monitor for individual stock comments.

Business Wire

http://www.businesswire.com

Power Index Categories	
Company Profiles	News By Company
EDGAR Access	Phone Numbers of Companies
News	SEC Filings

Use this site to find press releases issued by any companies you're following.

Business Wire's business is to get companies' full-text press releases out to the public. Remember that the press releases you read at this site were written by the companies themselves, and not by independent journalists. Companies will usually try to put the best spin possible on any news about themselves, so while the information presented here will usually be accurate, the analysis of what the information means for a company's future may differ greatly depending on who you ask.

Corporate News on the Net

Here you'll find press releases from scores of (but not all) companies, listed alphabetically, with a symbol to indicate which items are newly posted. Clicking on a company's name will get you links to current and historical press releases, plus a link to a current stock quote on the company (provided by DBC Online). To make things easier for you, the press releases are separated into categories such as:

- Earnings
- Management Changes
- Product
- Mergers/Acquisitions

If the company has its own web site, there will be a link to that as well.

In addition, some company pages have a convenient link that will send you to the SEC's EDGAR database and execute a search for the company's filings. You get to see the results of the EDGAR search without having to maneuver through the service yourself.

Electronic Media Kit

This area contains company information similar to that found in the Corporate News on the Net area. However, the list of companies in each area differs, so be sure to check both areas when trying to find information on a specific company.

Corporate Profiles on the Net

Here you'll find profiles for various companies (again, not always the same companies listed in other areas of the site). Check the "Published Date" to see how current the profile is. The profiles usually contain:

- the Public Relations Contact name and phone number (and sometimes e-mail address)
- the Industry Group
- a general description of the company's goods, services, operations and goals

There is also a link to the company's own web site if they have one.

Today's News on the Net

If you're looking for new ideas rather than information on a specific company, look here for hourly press release headlines with full-text links.

Business Wire Newsletter

Skip it. This is company news about Business Wire itself, plus general discussions of issues relevant to professionals in the "press-release" business. This area will contain little information of interest to you as an individual investor.

Retail Reports

Here you'll find the most recent sales figures for specific companies, broken down by industry segment such as:

- Specialty Apparel (such as American Eagle Outfitters, The Gap, Gymboree, Sunglass Hut)
- General Merchandise (such as Bradlees, Caldor, Dayton-Hudson, K-Mart)
- Home Supply (such as Bed, Bath & Beyond, Circuit City, Pier 1)

Chicago Tribune

http://www.webpoint.com/stocks/tribune

Power Index Categories	
12-Month Earnings	Market Cap
5-Year High & Low	Market Indicators
52 Week High & Low	Most Active Lists
Annual Dividend	Mutual Fund Information
Annual Yield	News
Biggest Gainer/Loser Lists	P/E Ratio
Currency Quotes	Quotes
Earnings Information	Quotes - By Industry Group
Earnings Per Share	Quotes - Currency
Exchange Rates	Quotes - Volume
Fundamental Stock Information	Symbol Searches
Last Week's High & Low	

The web location listed above is a fast back door route into the Chicago Tribune's stock section. The site can provide you with current quotes on most all of the major market indices, and also provides good historical and fundamental information (such as market caps) as part of their stock quotes.

Quotes

Symbol searches are available. Quotes are delayed (sometimes less than 10 minutes), and provide current and historical information:

- Open
- High
- Low
- Last
- Change from previous day's close
- Percentage Change
- Volume
- P/E ratio
- Last week's high
- Last week's low
- Last week's volume
- Last week's close
- Last week's net change
- Last week's percentage change
- Annual dividend

- Annual yield
- 12-month earnings
- Previous 12-month earnings
- 52-week high and low
- 5-year high and low
- 4-week net change
- Year-to-date net change
- 365-day net change
- Market capitalization (in 1000's)

Market Indicators

The main page also contains information on the Dow Jones Industrials, the NYSE Composite and the NASDAQ Composite indices. The following information is provided:

- Open
- High
- Low
- Last
- Net Change
- Percent Change

If you're not sure how one of these is determined, click on the title to see an explanation. Click on Market Indices at the bottom of the main page, and you'll find the same information for all of the various indices published by Dow Jones, Standard & Poor's, NYSE, NASDAQ and AMEX, as well as a number of other indices including the Internet Index, the Morgan Stanley indices, the Russell 2000 Index and the Value Line Geometric Index.

Mutual Funds

Here you'll get the latest closing prices on the 25 largest mutual funds. Quotes and symbol searches are also available for all funds. Fund quotes provide:

- Net asset value
- Offer Price
- Net change
- Percentage change
- Last Friday's net asset value
- 52-week high and low
- Year-to-date net change
- Year-to-date percentage change
- Annual dividend

New York Stock Exchange, American Stock Exchange, NASDAQ Stock Exchange

These three sections provide the following information for their respective exchanges:

- Indices
- Volume Leaders
- Percent Gainers
- Percent Losers
- current price of the 25 Most Widely Held Stocks

Be careful to check the time stamps of these screens; information is not updated constantly during the day. The information here can be over an hour old.

Industry Performance

Look here for lists of stocks by market sector for:

- Internet
- Financial
- Industrials
- Media
- Transportation
- Pharmaceuticals
- Telecommunication
- Semiconductors
- Gaming
- Basic Materials

Exchange Rates

Check here for a comparison of the U.S. Dollar with a large number of foreign currencies. They supply figures for both the foreign currency in U.S. Dollars, and U.S. Dollars in the foreign currency.

Current News

For news updates click on BACK TO PAGE ONE, then on News Briefs. This will provide you with national news headlines on general topics, and you can click through to the full stories.

CNNfn

http://cnnfn.com

Power Index Categories	
52 Week High & Low	Market Indicators
Articles	Most Active Lists
Biggest Gainer/Loser Lists	New High/Low Lists
Bond Data	News - Intraday
Bond Information	Personal Finance
Bond Quotes	P/E Ratio
Commodities & Futures Information	Quotes
Currency Quotes	Quotes - Bid & Ask
Dividends Per Share	Quotes - Closing Price
Earnings Per Share	Quotes - Commodities
Exchange Rates	Quotes - Currency
Greatest % Rise In Volume Lists	Quotes - Day's High & Low
Interest Rates	Quotes - Volume
International Market Indicators	Symbol Searches
	Volume Alert Lists

This is the web site of CNN's Financial Network cable channel. You'll find hot news and top stories listed right on the homepage for fast access. They also post current numbers for the Dow and the NASDAQ, plus an intraday chart of the Dow.

Hot Stories

This section provides today's headlines, plus full text time-stamped stories.

Markets

U.S. Stock Markets This area will provide delayed quotes on:

- Dow
- NYSE Composite
- NASDAQ Composite
- AMEX Market Value
- Standard & Poor's 500
- Dow Utilities
- Dow Transports
- Dow Composite
- Russell 2000
- the S&P 100 Index Options

For all 3 major exchanges, you can also view:

- Most Actives
- Biggest Gainers
- Biggest Losers
- New Highs
- New Lows
- Volume Alerts
- new 52-week highs and lows

World Markets Index quotes are updated at the end of each trading day for markets around the world.

Commodities Commodities quotes are delayed 20 minutes. For each type, CNN lists:

- Month
- Price
- Change

Interest Rates CNN posts intraday updates of U.S. Treasury Bills, and U.S. Treasury Notes and Bonds, showing Price, Change and Yield.

Currencies Here you can check to see how the U.S. Dollar is doing against a large number of foreign currencies.

Stock Quotes

Symbol search is available. You can get delayed quotes on stocks, mutual funds and money market funds. Quotes are time-stamped, and provide:

- Last price
- Change in price
- Today's open, high and low
- Previous Close
- Bid and Ask
- Volume
- P/E Ratio
- 52-week high and low
- Earnings per share
- Dividend per share

When you search on several symbols at once, the quotes are presented in separate groupings, rather than in one chart.

Your Money

Here CNN posts a number of articles of general interest to investors. For example, you'll find an explanation of compound interest, and advice on preventing thieves from destroying your credit record.

Corporate Financials Online

http://www.cfonews.com

Power Index Categories	
Addresses of Companies	News By Company
Earnings Information	Phone Numbers of Companies
Investor Relations Contacts	Quotes
Market Cap	SEC Filings
Market Indicators	Stock Ideas
News	

This site is an excellent source of financial/earnings information for a number of companies. CFO provides an arena for customer companies to post news releases and other information for potential investors (or any other interested parties). All of the company-specific information on this site is provided by the companies themselves. In addition, there are links to market newsletters with opinions and stock ideas.

Company News

Information is offered on a number of publicly traded companies, and they're all listed on the homepage so you can check quickly to see if the company you're interested in is there. Each company's name is a link that either leads to the company's own web site, or to information on the CFO web site. There are various categories of information that may be available for any given company, including:

- Latest News Releases
- Earnings News Releases
- Dividend News Releases
- Latest 10Q/10K Filings
- Shareholder Information

The earnings news releases and the SEC filings, when available, are an excellent source of hard numbers on companies.

Today's Company News

If you're looking for investment ideas, check here for the latest news releases listed by company.

The News and Observer

The News and Observer will provide you with the Top Story, stories on the Markets, and Today's Headlines relating to business.

Market Snapshot

This will give you the latest figures on the major market indexes.

Wall Street Opinion

Following this link will lead you to summaries of the latest information from a number of business publications, including:

- Barron's
- Wall Street Journal
- Bernie Schaeffer & Price Headley - Investment Institute
- S&P Market Scope
- Traders Faxline
- WORLDCO, LLC. "Dr. John Faessel on the Market"
- Hotstocks @ Streetlevel
- Wall Street Traders Column

Some of these include trade recommendations.

Quotes

Quotes are only available for spotlighted companies, and provide:

- Price
- Change
- Percent Change
- Volume
- High
- Low
- Bid
- Ask
- Open
- Industry Group
- Market Cap
- brief description of products and services
- company address, phone number and investor relations contact

DBC Online

http://www.dbc.com

Power Index Categories	
Premier Site	Market Commentary - Intraday
52 Week High & Low	Market Indicators
ADR (American Depositary Receipts) Information	Mutual Fund Information
Articles	News
Bank Rates	News - Intraday
Biggest Gainer/Loser Lists	News Feeds
Bond Data	Number of Shares
Bond Information	Options - Most Active
Bond Quotes	Options Information
Calendars of Economic Reports	Portfolio/Watch List Tracking
Charts	P/E Ratio
Charts - Daily	Quotes
Current Yield	Quotes - Bid & Ask
Dividends Per Share	Quotes - Bid & Ask Size
Earnings Per Share	Quotes - By Industry Group
Ex-Dividend Dates	Quotes - Day's High & Low
Fundamental Stock Information	Quotes - Volume
Getting Started	Rates - Consumer Loans
Global Investment & Economic Information	Rates - Credit Cards
Glossaries	Rates - Home Equity
Graphs (see also Charts)	Rates - Mortgage
Greatest % Rise In Volume Lists	Rates - Savings
International Investment Information	SEC Filings
Intraday Market Commentary	Shares Outstanding
Market Analysis	Stock Predictions
Market Cap	Stock Ideas
Market Commentary	Symbol Searches
	Volatility
	Watch List/Portfolio Tracking
	Yield

This site has an extraordinary amount of free information. It's well worth getting to know.

Quotes & Charts

The quote screen gives you the option of displaying prices in fractions or decimals. The date and time of the quote will appear at the bottom of each quote table.

Choose the Fast Quote option and enter up to 7 symbols to see:

- Last price
- Change in price
- Previous price
- day's Low
- day's High
- Bid
- Ask
- Volume

Choose the Single Fundamental option and enter a single symbol to see:

- Last price
- Currency (such as U.S. Dollar or Canadian Dollar)
- Change in price
- % Change in price
- Bid & Bid Size
- Ask & Ask Size
- Day Low
- Day High
- Previous price
- Volume
- 52-Week Low & High
- EPS
- P/E Ratio
- Dividend Amount
- Ex-Dividend Date
- Volatility
- Current Yield
- Number of Shares
- Market Cap

If you follow the link for help on symbol entry you'll also find a nice explanation of the differences between symbols for various types of investments (Indexes, Stocks, Commodities, Mutual Funds, and Money Market Funds).

From the same page used to obtain quotes, choose the Single Chart option, enter one symbol, and you'll get the standard Fast Quote information plus a 180-day bar chart with price and volume information.

DBC's charts include a 50-day moving average line.

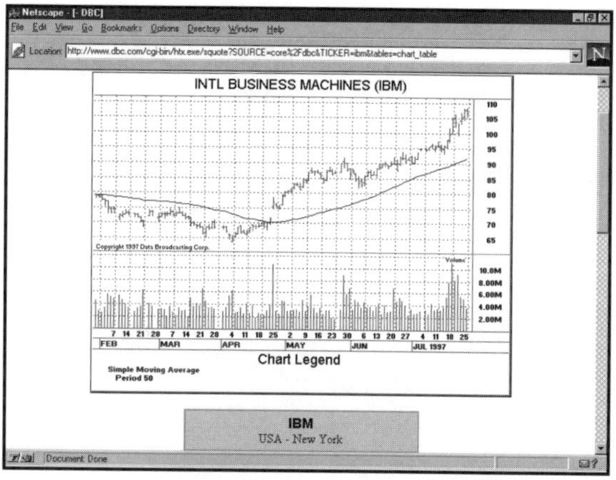

Financial Glossary

You can find this under Map of Site. A fairly sizable list of terms is posted here with explanations in plain English.

Symbol Search

You can search on U.S. Indexes, U.S. Commodities, Canadian Indexes, U.S. Stocks, OTC Bulletin Board Stocks, U.S. Mutual Funds, U.S. Money Market Funds and Canadian Stocks, as well as European Markets, Asian Markets, and South American Markets.

Personal Portfolio

This is purely a stock watch feature. You provide up to 7 ticker symbols, choosing from Stock, Mutual Fund, Money Market Fund and Index symbols. Then you can check the current quotes for all 7 symbols simply by referring to your "portfolio." Unlike a true portfolio tracker, it will not track the price you paid (or the market price when you started watching), or the number of shares held.

Financial Markets

Under Major Indexes, DBC provides you with a large number of market indices, giving you: the Last quote; the Change; the % Change; the session's High and Low; and the Volume:

Dow Jones Industrial Index
Dow Jones Transportation Index
Dow Jones Utilities Index
NASDAQ Composite Index
NYSE Composite Index
S&P 500 Stock Index
S&P 400 MidCap Stock Index
S&P 100 Stock Index

NASDAQ High Technology Index
AMEX High Technology Index
PSE High Technology Index
Morgan Stanley High Tech Index
Semiconductor Index
AMEX Major Market Index
Wilshire Small Cap Index
Financial Times-Stock Index
Mexico Index
10 Year T-Note Interest Rate (x .10)
30 Year T-Bond Interest Rate x .10)
PHLX Gold and Silver Index
Value Line Index (Arithmetic)
Value Line Index (Geometric)
Russell 1000
Russell 2000
Russell 3000

Industry Indexes will give you current updates on dozens of industry groups.

Most Active/Gainers/Losers (including options)—under the heading of each of the major stock markets (New York Stock Exchange, American Stock Exchange, and NASDAQ Stock Market), plus a separate section for Options, you'll find Top Ten lists for:

- Volume Leaders
- Percentage Gainers
- Percentage Losers

Newsroom

In the DBC Newsroom, you'll find a large number of links to follow to different sorts of information.

DBC Calendar will provide you with a list of the upcoming economic reports.

Today's Headlines is an important source of news, jam-packed with 1-line stories (it's harder to get more to the point). Each line indicates the time the story was released, and company names and ticker symbols are listed. The ticker symbols are quick links to current quotes.

Movers & Shakers will highlight fast-moving stocks and the stories behind them.

Futures Movers provides a narrative of the current action in the futures markets.

IPO Report provides a daily report on, you guessed it, upcoming initial public offerings of stock.

Two other features in the Newsroom, Earnings Surprises and Analysts' Changes, will highlight stocks that are likely to see action.

The Bond Quotes section of the Newsroom page will provide you with information on U.S. Treasuries, Corporate Bonds, Mortgage Bonds and CMO Bonds.

The Bank Rate Monitor link provides access to mortgage rates, savings rates in information on home equity, credit cards, consumer loans and banking.

In the Research section, you can access MarketGuide Reports on a large number of companies. Hoover's Company Capsules will provide you with a company description and some fundamental data. CompanyLink provides a mix of free and pay-per-view articles on companies.

In addition, the Weekly Scoops section of the newsroom contains lively and sometimes informative articles and features on investing.

Global Markets

This area provides information on international markets, stock indexes, foreign exchange rates and more. You can obtain information on American Depositary Receipts (ADR's) from:

- Argentina
- Australia
- Brazil
- Canada
- Chile
- Colombia
- Denmark
- Finland
- France
- Germany
- Hong Kong & China
- Indonesia
- Ireland
- Israel
- Italy
- Japan
- Luxembourg
- Mexico
- Netherlands
- New Zealand
- Norway
- Portugal
- South Africa
- Spain
- Sweden
- United Kingdom

Market Snapshot

This provides a narrative of what's happening in the market.

Direct Stock Purchase Plan Clearing House

http://www.netstockdirect.com/lists/ch.html

Power Index Categories	
Dividend Re-Investment Plans	No-Load Stocks
Offline Information	

This site will send you information by mail on no-load stock plans simply by checking off the information you want and providing your name and address. You can request up to 5 prospectuses at once.

The service is also available by phone at (800) 774-4117.

Netwise Tidbit

Netstock Direct

http://www.netstockdirect.com

This site provides information on more than 300 companies with direct stock purchasing plans.

Dividend Re-Investment Program Guide

http://www.cs.cmu.edu/~jdg/drip.html

Power Index Categories	
Dividend Re-Investment Plans	No-Load Stocks
Getting Started	Offline Information

This is a great place to start learning about Dividend Re-Investment Plans (DRIPs). You can learn all about what they are and where to go if you want to pursue purchasing stocks using DRIPs.

Dividend Re-Investment Plans offer a cost-efficient way to invest in stocks when you either (i) don't have a lot of money to invest, or (ii) want to significantly reduce or even eliminate brokerage fees for purchasing or selling stock. DRIPs are sometimes also called Shareholder Investment Plans. As this site will explain, some companies' plans require that you own stock in the company before joining the plan. However, many plans allow you to join with your initial purchase of stock; these are called No-Load plans.

There are basic variations in DRIPs, and this site will explain the differences to you in plain language. There is also a discussion of the advantages and disadvantages of Dividend Re-Investment Plans in general.

You'll also find a long (though not complete) list of companies offering Dividend Re-Investment Plans with the following information: the phone number; any discount to market value offered by the company when buying the stock; the number of shares you must own before you can join the DRIP (zero means it's a No-Load stock); and any other miscellaneous notes. You'll find that companies offering No-Load plans include: Dial, Exxon, Johnson Controls and Mobil.

Dorsey, Wright & Associates

http://www.dorseywright.com

Power Index Categories	
Premier Site	Point & Figure Charting
Charts	Stock Predictions
Charts - Point & Figure	Stock Ideas
Free Trials	Technical Analysis Information
Graphs (see also Charts)	

This site is all about Point & Figure Charting for a stock, bond, or other type of investment.

The Point & Figure method of charting is a way of analyzing the supply of and demand for a stock, bond, commodity, speculation or other investment. According to Dorsey, Wright, the method is also straightforward and easy to understand. While fundamental analysis will help you determine *what* to buy, Point & Figure Charting is a form of technical analysis that will help determine *when* to buy (and when to sell).

Start by going into the Recommended Reading section and reading the introduction to Tom Dorsey's book *Point & Figure Charting*, which you can access by clicking on the image of the cover. In addition, the site's Morning Call is a daily source of stock ideas.

DWA's Point & Figure Charting method can be used on stocks, bonds and other types of investments.

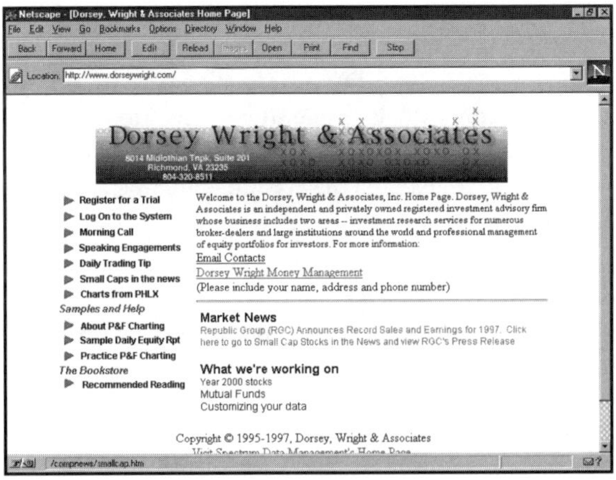

About P&F Charting

After you read the introduction to Dorsey's book, move on to your first lesson on Point & Figure Charting, with information on:

- Point & Figure Charting Basics
- Point & Figure Relative Strength
- Point & Figure Technical Indicators

There are also a number of example charts to view. If you're still a little confused about how this point & figure stuff actually works, the charting practice lessons in the next section will start clearing things up for you.

Practice P&F Charting

Once you've read a bit about it, it's time to try some charting. This section will lay out a typical chart, give you additional price information, and let you take a guess as to how to update the chart. Click on your guess to find out whether you're right or wrong. You can always backtrack to redo each exercise as you learn the basic principles.

Charts from the PHLX

Once you've started getting the hang of making and reading the charts, you can hone your skills further using examples of Point & Figure charts from the Philadelphia Stock Exchange. Pick a couple of stocks, predict future movements and track your results, or try charting a stock yourself and then comparing it to the version found here to check your technique. For example, print up a normal daily chart from, say, Quote.com (http://www.quote.com). Use the information in the daily chart to create your own Point & Figure chart, then check your chart against DWA's chart.

Morning Call

Click on See & Hear DWA's Morning Call for a free daily update featuring a discussion on a stock or two. It's worth it to download RealAudio (a free program that works with your browser — get it from http://www.real.com) so you will be able to listen to the commentary that accompanies the charts and written comments.

Daily Trading Tip

This area, updated regularly, offers a concise tip on Point & Figure Charting or investing in general.

Register for a Trial

For a free 2-week trial of research and charting available from Dorsey, Wright, click on Register and then Register As A Visitor. DWA will immediately send you a temporary password by e-mail, and they'll send you another notification when you can begin using the password you chose yourself.

Once you've registered, you'll have access to more information, including:

Small Cap Companies in the News This section covers small cap stocks that have caught Dorsey, Wright's interest. You'll be able to view a Point & Figure chart for the stock along with other information on factors such as relative strength and momentum. Any recent news is highlighted, along with a link to the company's web site, if there is one.

The DWA Online Bulletin Board System There are discussion forums for: Consumer; Cyclical; Financial; Health Care; Technology; and General. More forums are expected in the future.

Idea Generator This page continually updates itself to present current Point & Figure charts of stocks that have reached potential action points.

Point & Figure Charts Online From this menu, you can access the Point & Figure charts of a large number of stocks and mutual funds.

There is also a daily listing of Positive Earnings Surprises, and a weekly commentary to a financial magazine's stock picks, adding Dorsey, Wright's technical analysis to the magazine's story. In addition, you can access Point & Figure charts for a number of World Equity Benchmark Shares (WEBS), market indices and commodities.

DWA provides examples of Point & Figure charts in the site's practice area.

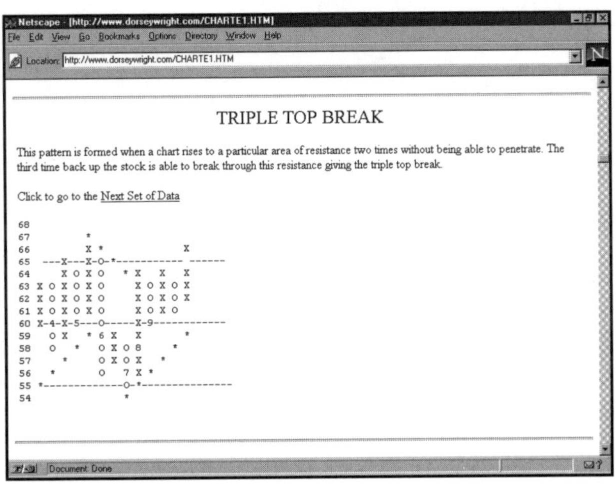

DRP IRA

http://www.drpira.com

Power Index Categories	
Articles	IRA Information
Dividend Re-Investment Plans	

This site contains excellent explanations and discussions of Dividend Re-Investment Plans and IRAs.

This site explains the benefits of combining 2 investment devices:

- Individual Retirement Accounts (IRAs), personal savings retirement programs that offer tax advantages to set aside money for retirement
- Dividend Re-Investment Plans (DRPs or DRIPs), plans offered by individual companies allowing consumers to buy stock directly from the offering company with little or no commission

You'll have to look at some of the other Dividend Re-Investment Plan sites covered in this book for lists of companies that actually offer DRIPs.

Netwise Tidbit

Green Jungle
http://www.greenjungle.com
Investment resources, including market commentary and mutual fund information.

Eanalytics

http://www.e-analytics.com

Power Index Categories	
Premier Site	Insurance Information
Answers to Questions (Free)	Investment Strategies
Appreciation Ranking Lists	Market Analysis
Articles	Market Indicators
Bond Information	Newsletters
Bond Quotes	Options Information
Calendars of Economic Reports	Options Trading Ideas
Commodities & Futures Information	Orders - Types of
Currency Quotes	Personal Finance
E-mail Lists	Quotes - Currency
Earnings Announcements Schedule	Retirement Planning
Earnings Information	Software Downloads
Exchange Rates	Software Reviews
Financial Planning	Stock Predictions
Futures & Commodities Information	Stock Ideas
Getting Started	Stock Splits
Glossaries	Technical Analysis Information
Government Reports Schedule	Worksheets - Cash Flow
	Worksheets - Life Insurance
	Worksheets - Net Worth
	Worksheets - Retirement Needs

This is an excellent site to visit to develop a beginning or intermediate understanding of any of the particular areas of investments available to individual investors. The worksheets available here will be especially helpful to anyone wanting to take a serious approach to financial planning and investing.

Free Weekly Newsletter

You need only provide your name and e-mail address to subscribe.

Financial Planning

A series of articles here will explain financial planning, and guide you through the initial steps of building a plan for yourself. Concepts include having an emergency fund and proper insurance. The Net Worth Worksheet can be printed out and will help you add up all of your assets and liabilities to give you a better picture of your financial condition.

The Cash Flow Worksheet will help you figure out your total income and compare it to your total expenses. The worksheet breaks down these broad concepts into specific categories, making your task easier since all you have to do is fill in the blanks. There are also short essays on the different types of insurance you may need, including a How Much Life Insurance Do You Need Worksheet (it will probably take a little research on your personal benefits to answer some of the questions on this worksheet). Other topics include:

- Debt Management
- Retirement Planning
- Mutual Funds (with explanations of common concepts and terms)

Stocks

Start out with Buying and Owning Stock - The Basics. There is an explanation of the types of orders you can place to buy stock, including limit and stop orders. Investment Categories of Common Stocks will explain what people mean when they talk about Blue Chip stocks, Growth stocks, Income stocks, Cyclical stocks, Speculative stocks, and Defensive stocks. There are also explanations of:

- The Difference Between Cash Accounts and Margin Accounts
- The Short Sale of Stock
- Traditional Formula Plans For Buying and Selling Stocks (Dollar Cost Averaging, Constant Dollar, and Constant Ratio)
- Historical Volatility and Implied Volatility (including a math lesson on how to compute volatility)

The Tutorials on Different Technical Indicators can be especially helpful, with explanations of Relative Strength, Moving Averages, Advance Decline Lines and a number of other indicators.

Options

This area may not have everything you've ever wanted to know about options, but it'll come close. A number of short essays will fill you in on the basics of puts, calls, calendar spreads, ratio call spreads and more. When you think you're getting the hang of it, look at OEX Trading Recommendations Published Daily. You'll also find these recommendations in the Market Commentary section.

Bonds

This area includes Daily Closing Numbers For T-Notes, T-Bills, T-Bonds. There are also basic explanations of the types of bonds available, including a discussion of tax-exempt bonds vs. taxable bonds.

Technical Analysis

Technical Analysis is what Equity Analytics does. A look at 10 Points For Beginning Technical Traders will give you some general guidelines for pursuing technical analysis as a method of investing (first and foremost, test your system on paper before trading for real). There is also a recommended reading list. You can send your question about technical analysis to Eanalytics@aol.com; answers are free, but there's no guarantee on how fast they'll get back to you.

Software Downloads

This section contains financial software for Windows, and add-ons for Omega TradeStation and SuperCharts, available free for downloading.

Futures & Commodities

Closing Numbers From America's Futures & Commodities Exchanges will provide you with:

- Symbol
- Change
- Last, High & Low
- Open Interest

Quotes are supplied from:

The Chicago Board of Trade
The Chicago Mercantile Exchange
Contracts On The Coffee Sugar & Cocoa Exchange
The New York Cotton Exchange
The New York Futures Exchange
The Commodity Exchange
The Kansas City Board of Trade
The Midamerica Exchange
The Minneapolis Grain Exchange
The New York Mercantile Exchange

They also offer charts of the contract specifications for futures contracts traded on each exchange, providing: Symbol; Delivery Months; and Trading Hours.

An Introduction To Futures And Commodity Trading This section will explain the origins, purpose and special lingo of this corner of the investment world, and also includes a discussion of basic trading strategies. Other articles in this section include:

- The Differences Between A Forward Contract And A Futures Contract
- Types Of Futures And Commodities
- Why End Of Day Settlement Isn't Always The Last Trade

For a mathematical theory on futures, look at the Capital Asset Pricing Model (CAPM). There are also explanations of:

- Calculating Forward Rates of Interest Using Current Spot Rates
- Currency Swaps - The Very Basics

- Asset Backed Securities - The Basics
- An Explanation Of 13 Week (90 Day) Treasury Bills

Insurance (& Retirement Planning)

As far as insurance goes, you'll find sections explaining:

- Disability Insurance
- Automobile Insurance
- Health Insurance
- Home Insurance
- Introduction to Life Insurance
- Term, Whole Life, Universal and Variable Life Insurance
- Single Premium Life Insurance
- Choosing Between IRA's and Life Insurance
- Umbrella or Excess Personal Injury Protection

You'll also find a helpful worksheet entitled the How Much Life Insurance Do You Need Worksheet.

This section also includes information on retirement planning. Follow How Much Money Will You Need When You Retire to find a Retirement Cash Flow Worksheet that will take you through your expected income and expenditures. They also explain such concepts as: Variable and Fixed Annuities; Individual Retirement Accounts; Keogh Plans; Salary Reduction SEPs (SAR-SEP); 401(k) Plans; and Social Security.

End Of Day Data

Daily Snapshot of the Major Market Indexes This will provide you with the Symbol, Change, Last, High and Low for the major markets. There is information on Volume, Advancing and Declining Issues, Volatility and Cumulative Tick. You can also see a Daily Snapshot of Sector Stock Indexes.

Daily World Currency Closing Numbers This section provides FOREX quotes: Symbol; Last Quote; Supplying Bank; Time and Date.

Eanalytics also provides ranked lists of stocks:

- Every Stock in the S&P 500 ranked by Stock Appreciation in 1995
- Every Stock in the S&P 500 sorted alphabetically with its % increase or decrease since 12/29/95
- Every Stock in the Dow Jones Industrials in 1996 sorted by its % increase or decrease since 12/29/95
- Every Stock in the Dow Jones Transports in 1996 sorted by its % increase or decrease since 12/29/95
- Every Stock in the Dow Jones Utilities in 1996 sorted by its % increase or decrease since 12/29/95

The Dow

Here is everything you've ever wanted to know about the history of the Dow, plus daily closing numbers on the various Dow averages.

Coming Earnings Announcements

This chart lists earnings reports expected out in the coming week and includes the street estimate and last year's numbers.

Weekly Gov't Reports

This is a simple list of which government reports will be released in the week to come.

Stock Splits

First take a look at the explanation of stock splits and related events under Stock Splits, Reverse Stock Splits, Cash and Stock Dividends. This is followed by weekly listings of announcements of stock splits giving you:

- company name
- ticker symbol
- exchange on which the stock is traded
- Amount (such as 2 for 1)
- Record Date (on which you have to own the stock to receive the benefit of the split)
- Payment Date

Software Reviews

Investment-related programs are covered here.

Glossaries

Here you'll find glossaries of terms relating to:

- Technical Analysis Terms and General Investing
- Financial Regulators and Institutions
- Monetary Policy
- Financial Regulators and Institutions
- Payment Mechanisms
- Foreign Banking
- Consumer Credit
- Securities Credit
- Options and Futures
- Bonds

E*TRADE

http://www.etrade.com

Power Index Categories	
52 Week High & Low	P/E Ratio
Brokers	Quotes
Brokers - Internet Trading	Quotes - Day's High & Low
Contests/Games	Quotes - Volume
Market Simulations	Symbol Searches

This internet broker also offers free quotes.

Quotes

Free quotes (dclayed 20 minutes during market hours):

- current price
- 52-week high and low
- P/E ratio
- day's volume
- day's high and low net change

You have to provide your name and e-mail address to get a quote, and you can only ask for one quote at a time. On a good note, however, when you go back to the quote request screen it retains your name and e-mail information, so all you have to re-enter is the new stock symbol for the stock you want quoted. In addition, the stock quote screen also offers the additional feature of searching for a stock symbol when all you know is the company's name. The quote screen does not provide the exact time of the quote as some other sites do, so you'll have to trust E*TRADE to stick to its 20-minute promise.

Free Stock Market and Options Game

Play the stock market with someone else's virtual cash.

Commissions

E*TRADE charges $14.95 for trades of listed stocks, and $19.95 for OTC stocks, including NASDAQ stocks. Trades can be requested using internet access, a touch-tone telephone system, or their own dialup BBS connection.

Fidelity Investments

http://www.fid-inv.com

Power Index Categories	
Articles	Getting Started
Brokers	Mutual Fund Companies
Calculators - Education Cost	Mutual Fund Information
Calculators - Investment Personality	Offline Information
Calculators - Retirement	Personal Finance
Contests/Games	Retirement Planning
Financial Planning	Risk Tolerance

If you want information on the mutual funds offered by Fidelity Investments, obviously this is the place. In addition, take advantage of the calculators for retirement and college costs.

Start by going directly to the Personal Investing area, where you'll find the following resources.

@82DEV

This area provides news and market data and articles on investing and investing concepts.

Investment Decisions

The Retirement Calculator will help estimate retirement needs and savings goals.

Investment Planning explains various types of investment plans, and offers a college cost calculator and an Asset Allocation Worksheet (to explore personal risk tolerance/investment personality).

Investor Toolbox leads directly to the various calculators that Fidelity offers:

- Retirement planning calculator
- College cost calculator
- Asset allocation worksheet (investment personality)
- Commission calculator
- Bond calculator
- Accrued interest calculator
- Credit card calculator

The Reference Room will lead you to Frequently Asked Questions area, as well as the Mutual fund reference room and an area on Tax-free investing.

Mutual Funds

This area contains information on over 150 Fidelity mutual funds. For each fund, they'll tell you about the fund's objective and strategy, the resume of the person managing the fund, and the fund's performance over the last several years compared to a number of major market indices. They'll also provide you with the fund's independent Lipper Rating, plus all fees associated with entering or exiting the fund. One interesting feature is a chart showing you the top 10 holdings of each fund. You can also access graphs of the Monthly NAV History of the fund, or of $10,000 Over Life of Fund. A prospectus for each fund is available for download.

Follow FundsNetwork Mutual Funds for information on funds (from many different companies) that can be purchased through Fidelity by Fidelity Brokerage customers. These listings contain some, but not all, of the information available for Fidelity funds.

Netwise Tidbit

Mutual Funds Interactive
http://www.fundsinteractive.com
Check out Funds 101 for the mutual fund beginner.

Holt Stock Report

http://metro.turnpike.net/holt/index.html

Power Index Categories	
Premier Site	Market Indicators
Advance/Decline Numbers	Most Active Lists
Currency - New Highs & Lows	New High/Low Lists
Currency Quotes	Optionable Stocks - Most Active
Gold Quotes	Optionable Stocks with New Highs/Lows
Greatest % Rise In Volume Lists	Optionable Stocks with Volume Increases
High EPS Growth with New High/Low Lists	Quotes - Currency
High EPS Growth & Greatest % Rise In Volume Lists	Volume Alert Lists
Interest Rates	

The Holt Report contains some helpful stock lists that one usually has to obtain by purchasing a financial paper such as Investor's Business Daily. For example, look for investment ideas in the daily list of stocks that have a high Earnings per Share growth rate and experienced a huge volume increase.

Most Recent Closing Report

A new report is posted here after each trading day with a whole lot of useful information:

- Market Indices & Averages (Open, Close, High and Low)
- Foreign Markets Indices
- Issues Traded (Advances/Declines/Unchanged numbers for each exchange)
- Currency (New Highs and Lows)
- Gold quotes
- Interest Rates
- Most Active stocks
- Stocks with Volume increases of greater than 50%
- Stocks that have reached a New High
- High EPS Growth Stocks with Volume increases greater than 50%
- High EPS Growth Stocks that have reached a New High
- High EPS Growth Stocks that have reached a New Low
- Optionable Stocks with Volume increases of greater than 50%
- Optionable Stocks that have reached a New High
- Optionable Stocks that have reached a New Low

Daily reports are easily accessible from the Holt homepage.

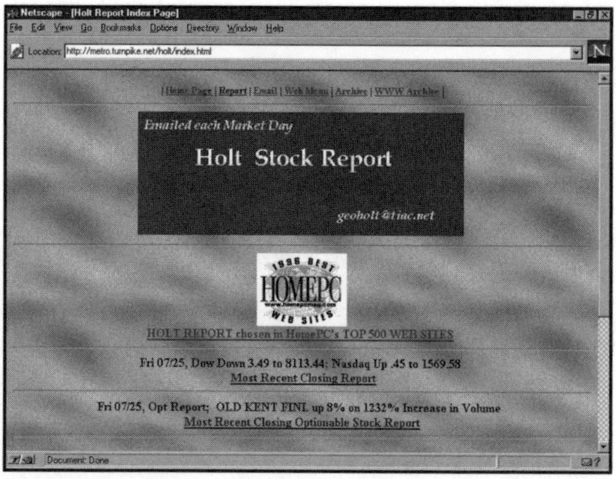

Holt Report WWW Archive

This is an archive of past reports listed by date.

Netwise Tidbit

The SmallCap Investor
http://www.smallcapinvestor.com

For the extremely risk-tolerant investor, a guide to investing in small and micro capitalization stocks.

Individual Investor

http://www.iionline.com

Power Index Categories	
Charts	News
Charts - Daily	News By Company
Company Profiles	Phone Numbers of Companies
Discussion Forums	Portfolio/Watch List Tracking
Discussion Forums By Stock	P/E Ratio
Earnings Estimates By Company	Quotes
Earnings Information	Quotes - Bid & Ask
Earnings Per Share	Quotes - Day's High & Low
Fundamental Stock Information	Quotes - Volume
Graphs (see also Charts)	Stock Predictions
Investment Strategies	Stock Ideas
Market Cap	Watch List/Portfolio Tracking

This is the on-line presence of Individual Investor Magazine. Since they feature a new stock every day, this is a great place to look for investment ideas. Individual Investor also offers extensive earnings estimate information from their quote screen.

Start by registering, which is easy, free and effective immediately. You choose your own password and username.

Stock of the Day

The Stock of the Day is posted on the top right corner of the main page. Click on the stock's name to see a current quote, plus an analysis of why Individual Investor thinks the stock might be a good investment opportunity.

Strategies (past Stocks of the Day)

To make things interesting, a different stock-picking strategy is used each day of the week. For example, Mondays feature stocks that have at least doubled earnings per share in the most recent quarter, and Thursdays look at companies whose shares have recently been purchased by company officers or directors (in other words, insider trading).

Click on any of the Strategy names to see an archive of past recommendations, including a comparison of the price at the time of recommendation and the current price.

Magic 25

Once a year, Individual Investor selects a portfolio of (you guessed it) 25 stocks that it follows for the next year. Check in here to see where those stocks have gone, and to get II's current recommendation on each stock (buy, sell or hold). Click on each stock's symbol to view II's analysis of the stock, and to check on when the current recommendation was made.

At the top of the page, you can also see whether the Magic 25 is beating the market. A simple table shows how the portfolio has fared against the Dow, NASDAQ Composite and the S&P 500 averages.

Market News

This is simple and straightforward intraday market news headlines, with full stories a click away.

Your Portfolio

Your portfolio will display:

- symbol
- cost per share
- number of shares
- total cost
- date purchased
- current price and change from previous close
- volume
- current value of shares held
- change in value
- percentage change in value

Forums

There are discussion forums on a number of individual stocks. If your stock isn't covered, you can drop in on the General Market Discussion forum and start a new discussion thread. You can also add a discussion conference on any topic.

Get Quote/Profile

Quotes provide:

- last sale
- net change
- day's high & low
- volume
- bid & ask
- 52-week high & low
- Trailing EPS

- Trailing P/E Ratio
- Market Capitalization

Click on Financials in Depth to see a Market Guide report for the stock, with a great deal of fundamental information including:

- various ratios and statistics
- share related information
- short interest information
- institutional & insider ownership
- growth rates
- historical quarterly results (revenue and earnings per share)
- address & phone number

Earnings Estimates provides extensive earnings information from I/B/E/S.

Company News will give you all of the recent headlines on the company (click through for the full stories).

Price Charts displays a 12 month price and volume chart. You can also select 3, 6, 24, and 26 month charts.

Choose SEC Filings from the quote screen and Individual Investor executes a quick search of the SEC's EDGAR database and displays a list of recent filings. Click on any filing to see the full text.

Netwise Tidbit

AlphaChart
http://www.alphachart.com
Free Java charts packed with technical analysis indicators like: Bollinger Bands, MACD, SAR, Momentum, RSI, and Accumulation/Distribution.

Infoseek

http://www.infoseek.com

Power Index Categories	
Premier Site	Most Active Lists
52 Week High & Low	New 52 Week Highs & Lows Lists
Biggest Gainer/Loser Lists	New High/Low Lists
Charts	News
Charts - Daily	News - Personalized
Charts - Moving Average Lines	News By Company
Charts - Weekly	Portfolio/Watch List Tracking
Company Profiles	P/E Ratio
Currency Quotes	Quotes - By Industry Group
Earnings Per Share	Quotes - Currency
Exchange Rates	Quotes - Day's High & Low
Fundamental Stock Information	Quotes - Volume
Graphs (see also Charts)	SEC Filings
Greatest % Rise In Volume Lists	Symbol Searches
International Market Indicators	Watch List/Portfolio Tracking
Market Indicators - Intraday Charts	Web Locations of Companies

Infoseek is a popular web search engine (you'll find a link to it on Netscape's web site), but it's also an information service.

From the homepage, click on Stock Quotes to get to the investment section.

Quotes & Charts

The quote screen actually provides access to both quotes and charts. You can enter several companies at once by symbol, but enter only one symbol if you want a chart. Symbol search is available. The delayed quote will provide:

- date and time
- opening price
- high
- low
- last
- percentage change in price
- volume
- earnings per share
- price/earnings ratio
- the 52-week price range

If you request a chart, your choices are:

- 50 Days
- 100 Days
- 200 Days
- 500 Days
- 1 Year (Weekly)
- 2 Year (Weekly)
- 5 Year (Weekly)

Here's a tip for Windows95 users. If you want to eliminate screen clutter and view the chart by itself, you can get a full-screen view of just the chart by right-clicking (clicking on the right-most mouse button) on the chart and choosing View Image.

Portfolio Tracker

Click on Portfolio Tracker to set up a new portfolio. In setting up your portfolio, you have the option of providing the number of shares, purchase date and purchase price. This will allow you to track the progress of the stock from a particular date and price. You will have the option of viewing your portfolio in terms of profit and loss, or in terms of fundamental information on each portfolio item.

Intraday Charts

This section contains intraday charts for the Dow Jones Industrials, the S&P 500 Index, the NASDAQ Composite and the S&P 100 OEX.

Stock Markets

This area provides the day's lists of stocks falling into the following categories:

- Most Actives
- Biggest Gainers
- High Alerts
- Low Alerts
- Biggest Losers
- Volume Alerts
- 52-wk Highs
- 52-wk Lows

Check out the bottom of each chart to see the exact time of the quotes.

Indices/Forex

This section contains same-day information on a number of market indices:

DOW JONES 30 INDUSTRIAL INDEX
DOW JONES TRANSPORTATION INDEX

DOW JONES UTILITIES INDEX
NASDAQ COMPOSITE INDEX
S&P 500 STOCK INDEX
S&P 100 STOCK INDEX
S&P 400 MIDCAP INDEX
AMEX INTERNET STOCK INDEX
MAJOR MARKET INDEX
WILSHIRE SMALL CAP INDEX
RUSSELL 2000 INDEX
PSE HIGH TECHNOLOGY INDEX
COMPUTER TECHNOLOGY INDEX
AMEX GOLD AND SILVER INDEX
FINANCIAL TIMES (FTSE) 100 INDEX
MEXICAN ADR INDEX
TORONTO 35 INDEX
VANCOUVER COMPOSITE INDEX
SEMICONDUCTOR SECTOR INDEX
13-WEEK TREASURY BILL INDEX
CRB INDEX
US DOLLAR INDEX
HANDY/HARMON GOLD SPOT
HANDY/HARMON SILVER SPOT

Index and Forex also contains a link to a list of the Dow Jones Industrials stocks with current quotes for each, and a Foreign Exchange link that will provide you with exchange rates for a number of foreign currencies:

AUSTRALIAN DOLLAR
BRITISH POUND
CANADIAN DOLLAR
DANISH KRONE
EUROPEAN CURRENCY UNIT
FINNISH MARKA
FRENCH FRANC
GERMAN MARK
HONG KONG DOLLAR
IRISH PUNT
ITALIAN LIRA
JAPANESE YEN
NORWEGIAN KRONE
SWEDISH KRONA
SWISS FRANC
HANDY/HARMON GOLD SPOT
HANDY/HARMON SILVER SPOT

Industry Groups

Industry Groups gives you current quotes of stocks grouped in the following categories:

- Internet Stocks
- Computers (PCs)
- Airlines and Aircraft
- Biotechnology
- Leisure Products
- Consumer Electronics
- Computers (Workstation)
- Computers (Networking)
- Computer Software

Company Profiles

Click on Company Profiles and you will be able to search a database of approximately 45,000 profiles.

The initial company profile will provide a brief company description, industry groups, address and phone number. Click on the News Stories button to perform a name search for current stories—some of the stories retrieved may have search words in common but not relate to the actual company in which you are interested.

For additional information, click on in-depth CompanyLink information. This will provide access to stock charts, SEC filings and recent news headlines for the company.

Newscenter

Clicking on Newscenter will take you to a main news page, which you can Personalize if you wish.

interactive nest egg

http://nestegg.iddis.com

Power Index Categories	
Calculators - Loan	Mutual Fund Performance Leader Lists
Calculators - Retirement	Personal Finance
Calendars of Economic Reports	Retirement Planning
Financial Planning	Tax Forms
Getting Started	Tax Information
Insurance Information	
Mutual Fund Information	

This is a good site for getting started with readings on mutual funds, stocks, bonds, etc. From the picture bar at the bottom of the homepage, select Education and go right to the subject index for a list of topics that may interest you.

Nest Egg Magazine

Nest Egg Magazine features stories relating to finance and investing. Subjects include:

- Retirement
- Insurance
- Real Estate
- Taxes
- College Savings

Mutual Fund Center

The Mutual Fund Directory offers an alphabetical listing of more than 9000 funds by fund family (company).

Top Funds provides lists of those funds with the Largest Assets and the funds that are Performance Leaders in the following categories:

- 1 Month Total Return
- 3 Month Total Return
- 1 Year Annualized Total Return
- 3 Year Annualized Total Return
- 5 Year Annualized Total Return

Clicking on a fund's symbol in each list takes you to a current graph and pricing data for that fund.

Reference Center

This area contains informative articles covering a broad range of topics:

- Cash & Credit Financing
- College Financing
- Employee Benefits
- Estate Planning
- Insurance
- Investments
- Real Estate
- Retirement
- Special Topics (including women's finance, divorce)
- Taxes

Planning Your Future

Here you'll find a retirement calculator, a loan calculator, and general retirement information such as Eight Common Mistakes in Retirement Planning.

Equity Center

This area provides a financial calendar, information on foreign and domestic markets, and lists of top equities (in terms of capitalization and most widely held).

IPO Center

IPOs are the center of discussion here, with lists of the best and worst recent initial public offerings, upcoming IPOs, and even an IPO contest.

Netwise Tidbit

AlphaCONNECT
http://www.alphaconnect.com

Download StockVue, free advanced portfolio-tracking software that uses your internet connection to continually obtain updated information from sources like Yahoo! and PC Quote.

Internal Revenue Service

http://www.irs.ustreas.gov/prod

Power Index Categories	
Premier Site	Tax Code (Federal)
Newsletters	Tax Forms
Tax Advice (Free)	Tax Information

Okay. Yes, it's the IRS, but anyone who leads off their online newsletter with the headlines like "Woman From Lake Calm Gets Off The Hook By Filing Her Taxes On-Line" can't be all bad, can they? In Tax Info For You, they'll actually answer some of your tax questions (and no, they don't ask for your name and social security number).

Tax Info For You

Start here. These are tax tips for individual filers. Tax Trails is an interactive tool that will answer a number of the most commonly asked questions by asking you specific questions, then providing the situation-specific answer for you. Questions include:

- Can You Claim a Dependency Exemption?
- Can You Claim Exemption From Withholding on Form W-4?
- Do You Have To Pay Estimated Tax?

The IRS with a sense of humor. Where else but on the internet?

Tax Regs in English

This includes a list of tax regulations issued since August 1, 1995, with references to plain language summaries where available.

IRS Newsstand

This news is mostly for practitioners rather than individual filers.

Forms & Pubs

The Publications here are the "official" IRS publications on various topics, such as "0295 Publ 1542 Per Diem Rates." Forms and Instructions will let you download any IRS form (and boy, are there lots of them) in one of four File Formats (including Adobe's popular PDF format). If you don't want to scan the lists, you can Search For A File.

Federation of Tax Administrators (FTA) provides links to state tax forms.

Need an extension on your tax deadline? Apparently, you're not alone. Click on Extensions for a short explanation of the rules and a quick link to obtain the proper extension form.

Netwise Tidbit

Federal Tax Code
http://www.tns.lcs.mit.edu/uscode

If your tax questions are so complex that you need to look here, then dig right in (and good luck!).

IPO Central

http://www.ipocentral.com

Power Index Categories	
E-Mail Lists	IPO Schedules

This is the place to learn about the Initial Public Offering market and look over IPO schedules.

Free Weekly IPO Update by E-mail

Tell them which parts of the IPO market you're interested in, and IPO Central will tailor a weekly e-mail update just for you.

IPO TIMETABLE

The timetable provides information on companies in all stages of the IPO cycle, including the latest filings, IPOs in registration, scheduled pricings for the coming week, aftermarket performance, withdrawals and postponements.

Beginner's Guide

Look here for an overview of the world of IPOs.

Netwise Tidbit

Pre-IPO News Bulletin
http://www.pre-iponews.com

Free e-mail bulletin lists high-tech pre-IPO companies going public on NASDAQ or OTCBB, ranging from $5 to $15 per share.

Lombard Institutional Brokerage Inc.

http://www.lombard.com

Power Index Categories	
52 Week High & Low	Ex-Dividend Dates
Average Daily Volume	Graphs (see also Charts)
Brokers	Links to Financial Sites
Brokers - Internet Trading	Offline Information
Calculators - Insurance	Options Information
Charts	P/E Ratio
Charts- Yearly	Quotes
Charts - Daily	Quotes - Day's High & Low
Charts - Intraday	Quotes - Option Symbol
Charts - Monthly	Quotes - Size of Last Trade
Charts - Weekly	Quotes - Volume
Dividend Yield	Symbol Searches

Starting at the Lombard homepage, click on Free Registration Desk to register for public access. To register, you will have to provide your name and a valid e-mail address, and choose a Login/UserID and a password. Although you must provide an e-mail address when you register, you won't receive a flood of e-mail messages or advertisements.

Once you've registered, from the homepage, click on the Public Access Center which offers the following free services.

Quotes

Using Lombard's Stock/Option Quote server, you can obtain a quote on a stock, option, mutual fund or index of interest to you. The quotes are delayed 20 minutes during trading hours. Information is available on over 7,000 companies. If you know the symbol of the company you're interested in, simply enter it and click on the Get Quote button. If you don't know the symbol for your stock, there is a Ticker Search function in the Chart area of the web site that will allow you to enter the company's name and search for the ticker symbol.

Information provided in response to a quote request includes:

- Last price
- Change in price from previous trade, and the percentage of the stock that the change represents
- current volume for the day

- date and time of the quote (this is the actual time of the trade quoted, as opposed to the time on the clock when you requested the information)
- size of the last trade
- opening price
- previous closing price
- the day's low and high price
- the ticker trend
- the option symbol
- the P/E ratio

Clicking on the company name in a quote screen will provide you with additional price and dividend information about the company:

- P/E ratio
- Average Daily Volume
- 52 Week Hi-Lo
- Calendar Year Hi-Lo
- Dividend Yield
- Last Dividend Amount
- Indicated Annual Dividend Rate
- Dividend Pay Date
- Ex-Dividend Date

There is also a link to the Option Chain page which will lead you to quote information on the various options (puts and calls) trading for the stock. The quote screen also has a link that will take you directly to the charting options for the stock you've quoted.

Charts

Lombard offers free Intraday and Historical charts on over 7,000 companies.

Choose from 4 chart sizes and 3 background colors. If you don't know the correct symbol, click on Ticker Search and use the company's name to search for the symbol.

The Intraday chart will give you the ups and downs of the current day's trading, minute by minute.

The historical charting feature is extremely versatile. You can choose to view recent trends in any number of days, weeks, months or years (the user determines how far back to go). In addition, you can select a 10, 50, 100 or 200 day moving average line to appear in the chart.

Each chart provide pricing (high, low and closing price) and volume information over the time period specified.

Research Links

Lombard's Public Access Center also offers links to other web sites in the following categories:

- Government
- Stock Information
- Mutual Fund Information
- Insurance Information
- Option Information
- Fixed Income-Bond and Interest Rate Information
- News and Periodicals
- Economic & Other Finance Information

Lombard Insurance Services

This area offers a searchable database of more than 1,500 term life and annuity plans from a number of insurance companies. The Estimator will use information you provide to calculate how much insurance you should have.

Brokerage Fees

Lombard is trying to get you to open a Lombard Account to access the site's premium services, allowing you to place realtime trades, view account information and gain access to realtime quotes for stocks and options. There are no account minimums or inactivity fees. Market Orders are $14.95, and Limit Orders are $19.95.

Offline

For free stuff on paper, call Lombard for an Information Packet at 1-800-LOMBARD (566-2273).

Netwise Tidbit

Gabelli Funds, Inc.
http://www.gabelli.com

Enter their free stock-picking contest. The winner gets 100 shares of Gabelli Global Multimedia Trust.

Mercury Mail Inc.

http://www.merc.com

Power Index Categories	
E-mail Lists	Quicken-Compatible Information
Portfolio/Watch List Tracking	Quotes - Closing Price

Mercury Mail offers a free daily e-mail service.

Closing Bell

You can choose to receive daily information on up to 30 stocks, mutual funds, etc., including price change and breaking news. You can also choose to receive information in Quicken or Excel/Lotus spreadsheet formats. Standard reports include:

- symbol
- security's name
- closing price
- price change
- trading volume

Their expanded report format adds:

- percentage price change
- daily high/low
- trading volume

Netwise Tidbit

Market Guide

http://www.marketguide.com

Their free Company Snapshot is a good place to start researching a stock.

The Motley Fool

http://www.fool.com

Power Index Categories	
Premier Site	Investment Strategies
Articles	Market Analysis
Calculators - PEG/YPEG (Fool Ratio)	Market Commentary
	News
Company Profiles	Offline Information
Contests/Games	Orders - Types of
Discussion Forums	Personal Finance
Discussion Forums By Stock	Rumors
Financial Planning	Software Downloads
Getting Started	Stock Predictions
Glossaries	

This is one of the best sites available on investing. Billed as "The Online Financial Forum For The Individual Investor," the site is run by the Motley Fools themselves, Dave & Tom Gardner (they also have a book and an area on America Online).

Overall, the site is designed to help personal investors obtain financial information and discuss investing techniques. And don't let the name fool you; these guys may not take themselves too seriously, but they are serious about investing. When they say "Foolish," they mean *smart*; Fools were the court jesters from Elizabethan England who were the only ones allowed to point out unpleasant truths to the King and Queen. In other words, these guys are trying to point out to you when the emperor isn't wearing any clothes. The Motley Fool stresses the importance of learning, intellectual integrity, long-term investing and humor.

If you're looking for specific information (about a company, for example), use Search the Fool to find information within the web site; it will search current and archived pages from the site.

On your first visit, try following What the Fool believes for a nice introduction and site tour.

The Fool's School

This is as good a place to start as any. The articles in this section will give you a taste of what the Fool's philosophy is all about. You'll find constantly changing articles and quizzes to learn about investing. There is also a Library of

Files which includes some downloadable programs for easily calculating some of the indicators used by the Fool in deciding which stocks to buy.

13 Easy Steps On The Foolish Path

These are a series of articles by various contributing Fools. This area is a great place for novices to learn about one point of view of stock market investing. They'll give you their opinions on the flaws of "conventional wisdom."

Here, you'll hear about strategies for getting your finances in order *before* you start investing: by saving regularly, erasing credit card debt, etc. They talk about choosing your first broker, and give suggestions on making your initial foray into the world of personal investments (such as investing in an index fund, buying stocks using the Fool's own simple Dow Dividend Approach, and investing for growth). They'll also tell you how to get and read hard copy investment information (for free), how to read an annual report, how to value growth stocks using the "Fool Ratio," and whether shorting stocks is for you.

The Dow Dividend Approach

This outlines one of the core strategies of the Fool, which is to buy the five worst Dow stocks (from the 30 stocks that comprise the Dow Jones Industrial Average), and hold them for a year looking forward to the (hopefully) inevitable comeback. There are three variations of the approach, one of which is called the Foolish Four. To find out which stocks are currently in the Foolish Four, just click on the Dow Dividend Approach.

Valuing Stocks

A series of articles here teaches how to determine the value of a company's stock, and how to spot undervalued stocks.

Of special interest is the PEG/YPEG Calculator, which will determine the Fool Ratio of a stock from information you supply. The Fool Ratio, which compares the Price/Earnings ratio to the Growth rate, is at the heart of the Motley Fool's stock-picking strategy.

Bust the Tipsters

This is a lesson and a game together. There is a new question every weekday, and prizes are awarded on a lottery system (the more you play, the more likely you are to win).

The Fribble

Drop by here for a daily essay that is short, opinionated, clever, logical, imaginative, amusing, joyous and interesting; at least in the opinion of the Fool.

The Portfolios: Fool & Boring

Check in on the Fool Portfolio and the Boring Portfolio. This information is more than just figures; they'll take you through the factors that played a part in deciding to add a particular stock to the Portfolio.

Lunchtime News/Evening News

Check here for a recap of the day's market activities, with winners and losers from the Fool's point of view. There are links to summaries of recent conference calls for various companies (where company representatives spoke with investment professionals about the future of the company), and a quick update on the Fool and Boring Portfolios.

Stock Ideas

If you're in search of a stock or two, try looking in Daily Double, Foolish Workshop, Industry Snapshot and Stock Screens.

Message Boards

This is where all sorts of visitors post their opinions, news, ruminations and any other tidbits about particular stocks or particular issues. Rumors, recommendations and apocalyptic warnings abound. Jump in and have fun.

The Fool FAQ

FAQ stands for Frequently Asked Questions, and this is a good place for answers to questions about:

- abbreviations
- Accumulation/Distribution
- Bid/Ask Price
- Initial Public Offerings
- Types of Orders, etc.

My Yahoo!

http://my.yahoo.com

Power Index Categories	
52 Week High & Low	Graphs (see also Charts)
Addresses of Companies	Market Indicators
Charts	News
Charts - Daily	News - Intraday
Company Profiles	News - Personalized
Dividends Per Share	News By Company
Earnings Estimates By Company	Phone Numbers of Companies
	Portfolio/Watch List Tracking
Earnings Information	P/E Ratio
Earnings Per Share	Quotes
Earnings Report Dates By Company	Quotes - Bid & Ask
	Quotes - Day's High & Low
Earnings Surprises By Company	Quotes - Volume
	Watch List/Portfolio Tracking
EDGAR Access	Web Locations of Companies
Ex-Dividend Amounts	Yield

This service allows you to create an individualized news summary page that you can bookmark and access instantly.

Start by clicking on the Start Your Own button to set up your personalized news page. During the setup process, you can add your initial list of stocks to track.

Quotes

When you access your personal news page, quotes for your stocks will be displayed in the top left corner, along with a number of major market indices. You can also request a quote on a new stock at any time using the window provided. Detailed quotes provide:

- price
- change
- previous close
- volume
- day's range
- bid & ask
- opening price
- ex-dividend

- 52-week range
- earnings per share
- P/E Ratio
- Dividends per Share
- Yield

Scroll down the quote page to see recent news headlines relating to the quoted item, with full stories available by clicking on the headlines.

Click on Profile from the detailed quote screen to view information such as:

- address, phone and fax numbers
- link to company's web site, if any
- number of employees
- annual sales
- company summary

Click on Research to see:

- number of brokers recommending (and level of recommendation)
- average recommendation (this week, last week and change)
- ranking in industry
- last quarters earnings
- last quarters earnings surprise
- earnings estimates (for this quarter, this year and next year)
- date next earnings announcement is expected

From the detailed quote screen, you can also access daily charts for the last 3 months, 1 year, 2 years and 5 years.

Click on SEC Filings to view a recent company filing, with links to a few more. While fewer reports are available here, they are formatted nicely for viewing with your browser.

NASDAQ

http://www.nasdaq.com

Power Index Categories	
Charts	Graphs (see also Charts)
Charts - Intraday	News
Charts - Monthly	News By Company
Complaint Filing Information	Quotes
EDGAR Access	Quotes - Day's High & Low
Glossaries	Quotes - Volume

NASDAQ, one of the three major stock exchanges, provides quotes from all of the big three exchanges, plus additional information on NASDAQ-traded companies.

Quotes

Quotes are provided for all three major exchanges, and include:

- Today's High & Low
- Last Sale & Net Change
- Previous Close
- Share Volume

NASDAQ Companies

Using this area as a launching point, you can access quotes, charts, company news, company facts and SEC filings for NASDAQ companies. The Charting options available are: Intraday; 3 Month; 6 Month; 12 Month; 24 Month; 36 Month; and 60 Month.

Company News provides headlines and full text stories from a number of news sources. SEC Filings will search the SEC's database for you and pull the results back to the NASDAQ web site for easy viewing.

Investor Services

Click on Protecting Investors for a list of trouble signs to watch for when dealing with brokers, as well as information on submitting complaints about questionable broker activities.

Reference

The Reference area contains general information about the NASDAQ exchange, plus a glossary of investing terms.

The National Association of Investors Corp.

http://www.better-investing.org

Power Index Categories	
E-mail Lists	Investment Strategies
Investment Club Information	Stock Ideas

The NAIC is a non-profit organization run largely by volunteers. NAIC's 3 basic investment principles are: (1) invest regularly over a long period of time; (2) reinvest the earnings that come from your investments; and (3) invest in companies likely to be worth more five years from now. You'll have to pay to become a member of NAIC ($39 a year) to get most of the information NAIC has. However, take a look at the free e-mail list for investors, as well as their list of the top 200 stocks owned by investment clubs across America.

Investment Club Info

If you're interested in Starting and Operating an Investment Club, NAIC has some online information (and offline info available for purchase). They'll also tell you where you can look for a club to join, or for people that might be interested in joining your own investment club.

Computer Services

NAIC has an E-Mail Discussion Forum you can join that includes discussion of stocks and industries under review by club members.

Learn to Invest

This mostly describes things you can buy from NAIC.

Company Information & Investing Ideas

Check out the Better Investing Top 200 to see a list of the 200 stocks most widely held by investment clubs nationwide.

NETworth

http://networth.galt.com

Power Index Categories	
Premier Site	Links to Financial Sites
52 Week High & Low	Market Analysis
Annual Dividend	Market Commentary
Canadian Exchanges - Quotes	Market Forecasts
Charts	Mutual Fund Companies
Charts- Yearly	Mutual Fund Information
Charts - Comparative Percentage	Mutual Fund Performance Leader Lists
Charts - Daily	Mutual Fund Profiles
Charts - Moving Average Lines	Mutual Fund Searches
Charts - Weekly	Mutual Funds - No Load Funds
Dividend Yield	No-Load Mutual Funds
Dividends Per Share	Portfolio/Watch List Tracking
Ex-Dividend Amounts	P/E Ratio
Ex-Dividend Dates	Quicken-Compatible Information
Fundamental Stock Information	Quotes
Graphs (see also Charts)	Quotes - Tickers
International Investment Information	Quotes - Volume
	Symbol Searches
Investor Relations Contacts	Watch List/Portfolio Tracking

Extensive mutual fund information and flexible stock charting are among the best of what this site has to offer. Be aware that there are sales pitches here and there among the hard information.

Register

Free registration is required to view some, but not all, of the information at this site. They ask for your name, address, phone number and e-mail address. You must also choose a username of 8 letters or less, and a password. If the username you submit is already in use, they will choose another similar one for you, which is somewhat annoying as it can be difficult to remember.

The Mutual Fund Market Manager

Market Outlook Look here for market commentary and economic forecasts.

Top Performers A menu here allows access to lists of top performing funds in a number of categories:

All Categories
Aggressive Growth
Equity-Income
Growth
Growth and Income
Europe Stock
Foreign Stock
Pacific Stock
World Stock
Specialty-Financial
Specialty-Health
Specialty-Natural Resources
Specialty-Precious Metals
Specialty-Technology
Specialty-Utilities
Specialty
Small Company
Asset Allocation
Balanced
Diversified Emerging Markets
Multi Asset-Global
Multi Sector Bond
Specialty-Communications
Specialty-Real Estate
Convertable Bond
Corporate Bond-High Yield
World Bond
Corporate Bond-General
Corporate Bond-High Quality
Govt. Bond-Adj-rate Mortgage
Govt. Bond-General
Govt. Bond-Mortgage
Govt. Bond-Treasury
Short-Term World Income
Municipal Bond-California
Municipal Bond-National
Municipal Bond-Single State
Municipal Bond-New York

There are six different lists for each category, each providing the best performers over a particular time frame:

- YTD (Year To Date)
- 3 Month
- 1 Year
- 3 Year
- 5 Year
- 10 Year

Fund Atlas This is a directory of presentations from mutual fund families (i.e., mutual fund companies). Choose the name of a fund family to obtain a fact sheet, net asset value, Morningstar Profile, or prospectus for each fund in the group.

Morningstar Profiles Enter a fund's symbol or name, and you'll be provided with a link to a Net Asset Value graph (if available), and the following information on the fund:

- Symbol
- Net Assets
- Morningstar Rating
- Objective
- Yield
- 3 Month Return
- 1 Year Rcturn
- 3 Year Return
- 5 Year Return
- Year To Date Return
- Fund Description
- Initial Minimum Purchase
- Subsequent Minimum Purchases
- Initial IRA Minimum Purchase
- Subsequent IRA Minimum Purchases
- Maximum Sales Charge
- Address
- Phone Number
- Portfolio Manager

Net Asset Values Enter a fund's name or symbol, and you'll get:

- NAV graph for the fund
- NAV's for the last 5 trading day's
- the 52-Week High & Low NAV

Fund Search This is a cross between a fund search engine and a screen, since you can can use certain technical information to filter out funds meeting specific requirements. You can search by Investment Objectives, fund category, or by a variety of fund performance and cost paramaters you can determine yourself.

The Equities Center

Company Research This area provides links to the web homepages of around 1800 publicly traded companies. Expect the list to expand as more companies take to the web.

I/B/E/S and Disclosure reports are for sale only. Skip them.

Quotes Quotes are delayed 15 minutes. Under Security Type, you can select a quote for: US Stock (the default); Toronto stock; Montreal stock; Vancouver stock; Can. OTC stock; Alberta stock; and Winnipeg Com. WCE.

Quotes provide:

- Last
- Change
- Day Range
- Previous Close
- Open
- Volume
- Tick Trend
- Market
- 52 Week Range
- Latest Dividend
- P/E Ratio
- Annual Dividend

For glossary explanations of any of these terms, simply click on the column heading of the term in question. Symbol search is also available.

Graphing Daily, weekly and yearly graphs are available. In addition, you can make a Comparative Percentage chart comparing as many as 4 securities; or you can choose a Price chart for a single security with 1 or more moving average lines (you can select 5, 10, 25, 50, 100 or 200 day moving averages).

Personal Portfolio You must be registered to use this feature. If you're entering this area for the first time, click on Create your customized Personal Portfolio. The portfolio allows you to track both funds and stocks. You provide: Symbol; Total Investment/Cost Basis; and Number of Shares. The portfolio's Default Configuration will display:

- Symbol
- Purchase Price
- Number of Shares

- Last Trade Price
- Change
- % Change
- Current Value
- Gain/Loss
- Gain/Loss %

The portfolio's Equity Fundamentals Configuration provides:

- Symbol
- Last Trade
- Company Name
- Market
- P/E Ratio
- Latest Dividend
- 52 Week High & Low
- Ex-Dividend Date
- Dividend Yield

If you have a Java-enabled browser, you can choose View Java Ticker from the Personal Portfolio Action menu to download a continually updating ticker tape of your portfolio prices. From the same menu, you can also download your portfolio prices to Quicken for Windows.

The Insider

This features links to financial sites, organized by general category.

Netwise Tidbit

Money Forum
http://www.moneyforum.com
Ask questions to a money expert, check out their investing and planning section, and join discussion groups.

No-Load Stocks Info

http://noload.base.org

Power Index Categories	
Dividend Re-Investment Plans	No-Load Stocks
E-mail Lists	

This site offers a list of stocks available for direct purchase (without using a broker as a middleman). The information varies from just a phone number to a somewhat detailed description of the plan and any fees. For example, according to the site, Dial Corp. will allow you to join their plan with a minimum investment of $100 with no fees at all. Exxon, on the other hand, requires a minimum investment of $250 plus "sales fee of $5.00 and commissions (plus taxes)."

The site also offers access to a No-Load Stock Plans E-mail Discussion List.

Netwise Tidbit

internet.com
http://www.internet.com
Internet news and resources, plus an Internet Stock Report.

NYU EDGAR

http://edgar.stern.nyu.edu

Power Index Categories	
Premier Site	Mutual Fund Holdings
EDGAR Access	Mutual Fund Information
EDGAR Information	SEC Filings

Don't even think of investing money in a company's stock without taking a look at its financial filings with the SEC. You can find those filings here. As an investor, you'll be especially interested in 10-Q Quarterly Reports and 10-K Annual Reports.

Many companies have been providing their SEC filings in electronic form for some time. However, since May 1996, all public companies have been required to provide their corporate SEC filings in electronic form so they can be added to the SEC's EDGAR (Electronic Data Gathering and Retrieval) database.

The EDGAR database is a gold mine for online investors.

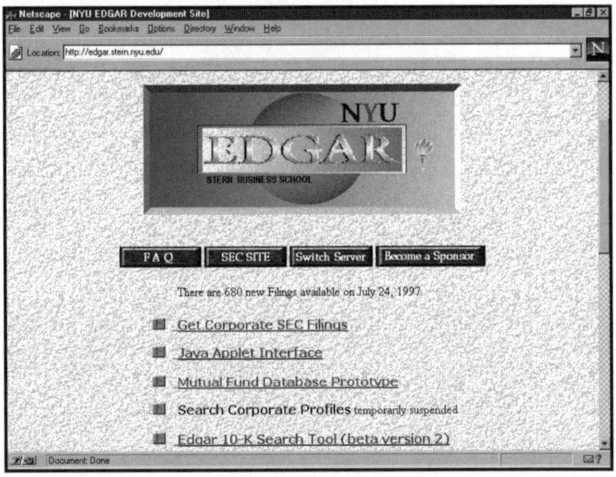

Get Corporate SEC Filings

You can search by ticker symbol, company name or by Zacks ticker symbol. Full text of all listed filings are available.

With the Company and Form Search, you can narrow your search by entering part of the company name, a date range of interest, and the type of form you want to retrieve (you can also enter "All" for Form Type).

There are also a number of other search types you can use, including a tool that searches exclusively for 10-K reports.

Mutual Fund Database Prototype

These reports allow the user to choose a Zacks Industrial sector and track movement through all quarterly filings. Only a few funds were covered at the time we visited (including many Fidelity funds), but they were planning on expanding the service. Pick a fund and an economy sector, and they'll tell you which stocks were held by the fund as of various reporting dates.

An EDGAR search will turn up all of the SEC filings from a company.

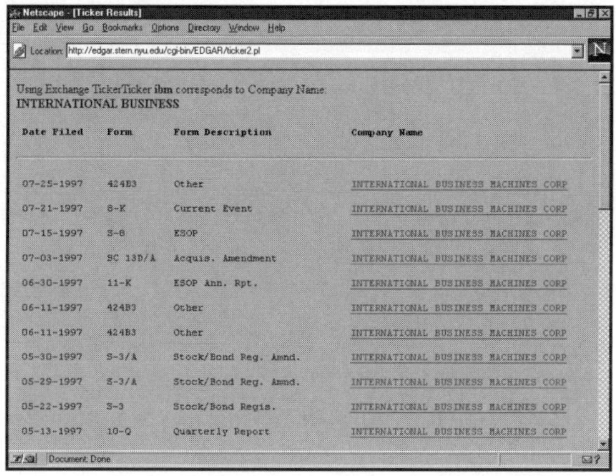

Netwise Tidbit

Understanding Financials
http://www.ibm.com/FinancialGuide

IBM provides this basic introduction to reading the financial statements in a company's annual report.

Pathfinder

http://pathfinder.com

Power Index Categories	
52 Week High & Low	Market Indicators
Articles	Mutual Fund Information
Calculators - Budget	News
Calculators - Mortgage	P/E Ratio
Calculators - Retirement	Quotes
Company Profiles	Quotes - Bid & Ask Size
Dividends Per Share	Quotes - Day's High & Low
Earnings Per Share	Quotes - Volume
EDGAR Access	Savings
Fundamental Stock Information	Symbol Searches
Getting Started	Web Locations of Companies

This site has news and other information from multiple sources, including Time, CNN, Money and Fortune. Look for other features to be added in the future.

Start by going to Quick Quotes, and link to other information from the menu there.

Quick Quotes

Symbol search is available. You can request a number of quotes at once. Each quote provides:

- Time of quote
- Open
- High
- Low
- Last
- Change
- Volume
- Earnings per Share
- P/E Ratio
- Dividends per Share
- 52 Week High/Low
- Bid & Ask (if applicable)

Quotes are delayed by 15 minutes.

Once a quote is displayed, click on the company name to additional information about the company, including:

- a description of the company's operations
- when the company's fiscal year ends
- last year's total sales
- the percentage change in last year's sales
- number of employees
- web site location

From this screen, a search of the Pathfinder web site will turn up articles referencing the company from such sources as Fortune, Time and Reuters. Following the SEC Filings link will execute a search for corporate filings on the SEC's EDGAR database.

Marketwatch

Major Indexes provides intraday graphs of the Dow Jones, S&P 500 and NASDAQ averages. If the average is up for the day, a special chart will indicate whether it's an average up day, a good day, or the best day in 10 years. A similar chart helps judge the severity of down days.

U.S. Exchanges provides similar views of NYSE, AMEX and NASDAQ. Other Indexes provides a table of basic information on:

- Dow Jones Industrial Average
- S&P 500
- NASDAQ Composite
- NYSE Composite
- Amex Market Value
- S&P 100
- Russell 2000
- MAJOR MARKET INDEX
- VALUE LINE COMP SECTOR INDEX
- Wilshire Smallcap

Money Online

This is Money Magazine's online home.

News Money Daily covers issues likely to affect personal finances. The Money Business Report provides daily updates on the market, recent economic reports and company earnings reports. Headlines provides major business news from Reuters.

Goals College goals leads to advice on saving for college, including a college cost calculator. There is information on college costs and how to pursue scholarship money. The Money College Guide provides details and rankings of over 1100 schools. There is even a search engine to help you Find Your Best College, using 8 general factors or 41 specific factors. General information available in this section will help you find the best rates on borrowing, saving and credit cards, reduce your debt, and use a calculator to determine the total or annualized return on any of your current investments.

Home goals include advice on cutting costs of the typical homeowner, a Mortgage Calculator, and an Instant Budget Maker to calculate expenses and compare them to average budgets of people with similar profiles. Find out which charities get the most out of each dollar contributed with the Charity Selector. There's even a special section for Women and Money.

Investing includes market analysis and articles on mutual funds. Of special interest are the articles on 7 Internet Investing Myths and the 12 Deadly Fund Myths. Get a financial life offers advice on personal finance for people in their twenties and thirties, while the Retirement Savings Calculator takes a look forward to the retirement years.

There are also areas on Retirement (including a Mutual Fund IQ Test), Savings and Borrowing and Taxes.

Fortune Online

This is, well, Fortune magazine online. 'Nuff said.

Netwise Tidbit

Mutual Funds Magazine
http://www.mfmag.com

Read current and back issues of the magazine, and subscribe to a free weekly e-mail newsletter.

PC Financial Network

http://www.pcfn.com

Power Index Categories	
52 Week High & Low	Market Indicators - Intraday Charts
Articles	Most Active Lists
Biggest Gainer/Loser Lists	Mutual Fund Information
Brokers	Mutual Fund Searches
Brokers - Internet Trading	News
Charts	News - Intraday
Charts - Comparative Percentage	News - Searchable
Charts - Daily	News By Company
Charts - Intraday	No-Load Mutual Funds
Charts - Monthly	Options Information
Charts - Moving Average Lines	Portfolio/Watch List Tracking
Charts - Weekly	P/E Ratio
Earnings Per Share	Quotes
Getting Started	Quotes - Bid & Ask
Glossaries	Quotes - Day's High & Low
Glossaries - Mutual Fund Terms	Quotes - Volume
Graphs (see also Charts)	Watch List/Portfolio Tracking
Market Indicators	Yield

Most of the information at this site is accessible from the pull down menu on the homepage. The charts offer a nice degree of customization, and the Pre-Market and Post-Market news coverage is great for news junkies who like to follow stock movements even when the markets are closed.

Quote - Stock (delayed)

The Extended Quote provides:

- price
- change
- volume
- bid & ask
- bid & ask size
- open
- close
- day's high & low
- 52-week high & low

- dividend
- P/E ratio
- Earnings per Share
- Yield

Click on Option List from the Extended Quote screen to see a list of puts and calls available for the symbol.

If you want to check quotes during the day without leaving whatever web site you are visiting at the time, click on the Remote Quote button on the PCFN homepage to open a separate quote window you can use at any time.

Quote - Mutual Fund

Each mutual fund quote provides the Net Asset Value as of the previous day's close, the change in price and the offer price.

Quote - Option (delayed)

If you don't know the specific option symbol, get a stock quote and then choose Option List to see all of the options available for a stock. The option quote screen provides:

- price
- bid & ask
- change
- volume
- open
- close
- open int.
- high
- low
- CHigh
- CLow
- Charts (gif)

PCFN's charting options are extensive. The time periods to choose from are:

- Intra-day every 5 minutes
- 1 week every 15 minutes
- 1 month daily
- 3 month daily
- 1 year weekly
- 3 year monthly
- 5 year monthly
- 10 year monthly

You can also compare the performance of a stock or fund against other stocks or funds, or against the following market indices:

- S&P 500
- S&P 100
- Dow Jones Industrials
- NYSE Composite
- NASDAQ Composite
- AMEX Composite
- Russell 2000

Display preferences for charts include:

- volume chart
- high/low/last lines
- gridlines
- 50 or 200 day moving average lines (or none at all)

You can also choose to receive charts in ActiveX/Plugin form. This will require downloading an add-on program for your Netscape Navigator or Microsoft Internet Explorer browser, but in the long run will enable you to download charts faster from PCFN.

News - All Sources

Enter a symbol for recent related news headlines. Click on any headline to display the full story. In the left column menu, you will also find links to:

- Search the News (for word searches)
- Industry News (you pick the industry)
- Market Headlines (the Pre-Market and Post-Market Coverage can give you a jump on the trading day)
- Research Headlines (with Research Alerts, Earnings Results and Earnings Forecasts)

Market Monitor

This page provides you with current levels for a number of market indices, plus an intraday graph of the Dow. The Market Monitor page also displays the current top 10 active stocks, plus intraday financial news headlines (with full stories available) from Reuters. From the left menu, you can also access lists of Percentage Winners and Percentage Losers. On the same menu you'll also find specialized news lists for IPO Highlights, Offerings and Mergers & Acquisitions.

Research & Ideas

S&P's How to Invest is a well-organized series of articles on the basics of investing, broken down into sections entitled: Why invest?; Physical and Financial Assets; Getting Started; Stocks; Fixed-Income Investments; Mutual Funds; and Brokers and Securities Markets. There is also a Glossary.

The PCFN FundCenter contains information on over 5,000 funds. PCFN FundScan allows you to screen those funds. The FundScan has fewer variables than some other fund screens, but that also makes it a little less daunting to use. You can use any or all of the following criteria:

- Fund Company
- Fund Objective
- Expense Ratio
- Relative Risk
- Relative Size
- Load/Fee Structure
- Manager Tenure
- Average Annual Performance

The Fund Glossary available here is fairly extensive.

Portfolio

You can create up to 20 Model Portfolios, each tracking up to 20 securities. Follow Free PCFN Services For PCFN Visitors, then click on Customized Model Portfolios.

Choose Display Portfolios, then select a display format. The Performance Data display will provide:

- symbol
- quantity
- current price
- purchase price
- gain or loss
- current value

The Quote Data display provides:

- price
- bid & ask
- change
- volume

Click on the any symbol to access a quote or extended quote for the security.

Brokerage Fees

PCFN charges $39.95 for a typical on-line trade. Accounts can be opened on-line, and some accounts can be approved for trading immediately even before an initial deposit is made.

PC Quote

http://www.pcquote.com

Power Index Categories	
52 Week High & Low	News By Company
Advance/Decline Numbers	Number of Shares
Charts	Options - Most Active
Charts - Daily	P/E Ratio
Charts - Moving Average Lines	Portfolio/Watchlist Tracking
Current Yield	Quotes
Dividend Frequency	Quotes - Bid & Ask
Dividends Per Share	Quotes - Bid & Ask Size
Earnings Per Share	Quotes - Day's High & Low
Ex-Dividend Dates	Quotes - Option Symbol
Fundamental Stock Information	Quotes - Volume
Graphs (see also Charts)	Shares Outstanding
Market Indicators	Software Downloads
Market Indicators - Intraday Charts	Symbol Searches
	Volatility
Mutual Fund Information	Watch List/Portfolio Tracking
News - Searchable	Yield

PC Quote's main product is a software suite of "dynamic realtime trading tools" that uses market data purchased from PC Quote and downloaded over the internet in realtime. To lure customers to the site, they provide delayed quotes plus some fundamental information, charts and news by company. They also offer free software to download that will use free information from PC Quote to track portfolios.

Markets at a Glance

The current level and net change for the day are displayed for a number of market indicators:

- DJIA
- Nasdaq Comp
- S&P 500
- S&P 100
- DJ Utilities
- $ Index Spot
- NYSE Comp
- Nikkei

- DJ Transports
- Russell 2000
- Semiconductor
- Internet Index

QuickQuote

Quotes are delayed approximately 20 minutes. A Detailed Quote provides:

- Last Sale (including whether the sale was a downtick or uptick)
- Net Change
- Exchange
- Time of Last Sale
- Size of Last Sale
- Bid & Ask
- Size of Bid & Ask
- Open
- High
- Low
- Volume
- Previous Close
- 52 Week High
- 52 Week Low
- Volatility
- Ex-Dividend Date
- Dividend Amount
- Dividend Frequency
- Earnings per Share
- P/E Ratio
- Yield
- Shares Outstanding (in 1000's)

Symbol search is available if you only know the company's name.

Choose Latest News from the QuickQuote menu to view headlines of stories concerning the company, from sources such as PRNewswire and Reuters. The full text of each story can be accessed by clicking on the story headline.

Choose Chart on the QuickQuote menu to access PC Quote's adjustable charting menu. Adjustable chart features include:

- Type of Chart (Bar, Line or Candle)
- 5 Chart sizes
- Start Date
- End Date
- Up to 3 moving average lines displayed at once (choose from 5, 10, 20, 25, 50, 100 and 200 day moving average lines)
- Logorithmic or non-logrithmic price scale

MarketSmart Delayed

This area is most easily accessed from a menu at the bottom of the homepage. Log in (it's free) for access to additional financial information.

Quote Watch will create and save groups of quotes to access in portfolio-like tables. The Quote Watch tables display:

- Last Sale
- Net Change
- Time of Last
- Bid
- Ask
- Bid & Ask Size
- Open
- High
- Low
- Volume

Options Watch will display the following information for all puts and calls being traded on an individual stock:

- Last Sale
- Net
- Bid
- Ask
- Volume
- Open Int

TopTen Watch will provide the 10 most active, 10 most up in price and 10 most down in price from the following:

- New York Stock Exchange
- New York Stock Exchange Options
- American Stock Exchange
- American Stock Exchange Options
- Boston Stock Exchange
- Cincinnati Stock Exchange
- Chicago Board Options Exchange
- NASDAQ
- Pacific Exchange
- Pacific Exchange Options
- Philadelphia Stock Exchange
- Philadelphia Stock Exchange Options

Chart Watch provides access to the same charting features described above under QuickQuote.

Portfolio Watch allows tracking of up to five portfolio of twenty symbols each.

This true portfolio feature will track the actual and percentage gain or loss from the "purchase" price entered when the symbol is added.

Currency Watch provides currency futures prices from the Chicago Mercantile Exchange.

Fund Watch provides an alphabetical listing of fund families, then a table with basic quote information for each fund in a particular fund family.

Index Watch provides quotes on a fairly comprehensive list of market indices.

Statistics Watch contains a number of unusual statistics, including:

- London Gold Fix
- S&P Spread (Difference Between the Near Month and Index of S&P 500)
- The TICK for Dow Composite Composite Index
- The TICK for the Dow Jones Industrial Average
- The TICK for the Dow Jones Transportation Index
- The TICK for the Dow Utility Index
- American Volume on Regional Exchange (shows the volume of issues whose primary exchange is the American Stock Exchange on the named exchange) for the Boston, Cincinnati, Chicago, Pacific, Philadelphia and NASDAQ exchanges.
- New York After Hours Trading Volume
- Block Trades (5000 shares and greater) for NYSE, AMEX and NASDAQ
- Odd Lot Sales at NYSE
- Dow Jones Average of 10 Industrial Bonds
- New Highs, Lows & Unchanged for NYSE, AMEX and NASDAQ

Market Watch throws out a lot of data at once to provide a snapshot of the markets, including:

- the most active, most up and most down of the Dow Jones stocks, the NASDAQ Composite and the AMEX
- quotes on major market indices, including the Russell 2000 and the NIKKEI (Tokyo)
- NYSE Advancing Issues
- NYSE Declining Issues
- NYSE Up Volume
- NYSE Down Volume
- NYSE Issues Traded
- Treasury Coupon quotes

Stock and Option Update provides information on new initial public offerings, stock changes, stock splits and options changes, updated on a daily basis. PC Quote's database can be searched for changes happening soon, or historically for changes that occurred within a set date range.

News Alert's database can be searched by term or by ticker, with full articles available. The time period of each search can be customized, and most recent news items are displayed first in search results.

Fixed Income Watch provides quotes on:

- Federal Funds
- Treasury Bills
- Mortgage-Backed Securities
- Cds
- Repos
- LIBOR
- Treasury Coupons
- Commercial Paper
- Bankers Accept.
- Bank Rate (Prime Rate)

BackWeb is a free downloadable program that, when linked with free delayed-time information from PC Quote, can track a customized portfolio and also provide:

- Scrolling Ticker Flashes
- Market Summary Flashes
- Company Update Flashes
- Top Ten Flashes
- High/Low Limit Flashes

Inside Track Micro Edition is another free software program that will track portfolios and news with free information from PC Quote.

Netwise Tidbit

Silicon Investor
http://www.techstocks.com
StockTalk features active discussion forums on tech companies.

Prudential Securities

http://www.prusec.com

Power Index Categories	
Premier Site	Market Commentary
Articles	Market Commentary - Intraday
Bond Information	Market Indicators
Brokers	Mutual Fund Companies
Brokers - Information	Mutual Fund Profiles
Calculators - Investment Personality	Newsletters
Calculators - Retirement	Offline Information
Financial Planning	Portfolio Management Concepts
Getting Started	Retirement Planning
Glossaries	Risk Tolerance
Investment Strategies	Seminars (Free)

Prudential Securities is a full-service broker, which means they're happy to give information away for free in the hopes that you'll become a client in the future. They consider their web site their "virtual branch office." Accordingly, they treat every visitor as a prospective customer—they want to provide you with helpful information *and* convince you to open an account with them.

If you're getting started, be sure to check out their Investment Personality Quiz and their retirement calculator.

Life's Financial Concerns

Investment Personality Quiz A study funded by PruSec found that 4 psychological traits influence a person's financial-planning and investment activities: assertiveness; flexibility; risk tolerance; and future orientation. To find out where you fit in, take their Personality Quiz. The quiz is anonymous, and presents a number of statements that imply certain attitudes about investing and life. You indicate whether or not each statement describes the way you feel or act. When you submit your answers, you receive a numerical score that fits into one of several categories of investors: the Caution Zone; the Comfort Zone; and the Action Zone.

PruSec explains what each zone means, and suggests different courses of action depending on which zone you're in, including links to other areas of PruSec's web site. For example, recommendations for people in the Caution Zone include:

- subscribe to a popular financial publication
- before you begin investing, build a reserve of 3-6 months' income that can be used for emergencies
- take inventory of your assets and liabilities to determine your net worth

By providing you with different links in each zone section, PruSec helps you tailor your use of its web site in accordance with your investment personality.

Retirement Calculate retirement savings needs with PruSec's Wealth Accumulation Calculator. PruSec has a somewhat different approach to retirement calculators. They see retirement planning as an equation involving 6 distinct variables:

- Amount of Current Investments
- Contribution Amount
- Frequency of Contribution and Compounding
- Annual Rate of Return on Investments
- Number of Years To Reach Your Goal
- Investment Goal (in dollars)

Their calculator lets you leave any one of these variables blank and fill in the other five. This lets you run the calculator a number of times to see how different changes in your investment plan will affect the outcome at your retirement. You may determine that increasing your monthly investment contribution by a modest amount may have a significant result over time.

Other topics covered here include:

- What Is an Individual Retirement Account?
- Company-Sponsored 401(k) Retirement Plans
- Frequently Asked Questions About IRAs

Children, Parents, Health, Spouse... Other areas here cover general topics that should be considered by any personal investor:

- planning for your children's education
- helping your parents through their golden years
- the health of your spouse
- your business
- taxes
- lifestyle (ah, yes, lifestyle)
- retirement

Each article has useful information, along with a pitch to contact your local PruSec Financial Advisor.

Financial Marketplace

Once you're in this area, click on Today's Market Commentary in the graphic at the top of the page to get to the first subsection.

Market Commentaries Each trading day, PruSec posts intraday comments on the markets.

The Pre-Opening Stock Market Commentary is posted about 8:30 a.m. Eastern time each morning, and will tie in such information as general market data, breaking news and earnings reports expected during the day. The Mid-Session Stock Market Commentary is posted around noon, and includes reports of sharply moving stocks. The Closing Stock Market Commentary is released sometime after 5:00 p.m.

The Opening Bond Market Commentary is posted around 10:00 a.m. Eastern time. The afternoon bond commentary is posted at around 1:30 p.m., and the closing commentary is posted around 5:30 p.m.

There are Treasury Market Commentaries as well.

Strategy Weekly This magazine is not available online, but a few excerpts from the latest issue are posted here. Free copies can also be requested.

Order Publications These publications are not available online, but you can order them for free. They include:

- Dow 7000: An End-of Decade Technical Forecast
- Prudential Securities' Single Best Equity Ideas
- Defining Your Financial Goals

Market Data Information in this area is updated once a week, on Thursdays. Data is available for:

- Market Indices
- Money Rates
- Treasury Bills, Notes & Bonds
- Treasury-Backed Zero Coupon Bonds—STRIPS
- Municipal Triple-A Rated General Obligation Bonds
- Corporate Bonds Triple-A Rated
- Preferred Stock
- GNMA Pass-Through
- Fixed-Rate Annuities
- 5-Year Foreign Currency Bond Yields

Investing and Investments

Investment Strategies Articles in this area discuss:

- Dollar-Cost Averaging
- Laddering a Fixed-Income Portfolio
- Socially Conscious Investing

Investing in Stocks and Bonds Articles on stocks include:

- Why Invest in Equities?
- Different Kinds of Stocks
- Nine Common Mistakes to Avoid When Investing in Equities
- International Equities

Articles on bonds include:

- Why Invest in Fixed-Income Securities?
- U.S. Treasury Securities
- Municipal Bonds
- Certificates of Deposit
- Zero-Coupon Bonds
- Mortgage-Backed Securities

Retirement Planning and More Plan for Your Retirement will lead you to an introduction to retirement issues, and a link to PruSec's retirement calculator. Other articles here include:

- What Is an Individual Retirement Account?
- Frequently Asked Questions about IRAs
- What a Prudential Securities IRA Can Do for You
- Company-Sponsored 401(k) Plans
- How to Give Securities to Minors: How UGMA and UTMA Rules Work
- What Is a Living Trust?
- What Is a Charitable Remainder Trust?

Prudential Mutual Funds This area features information about Prudential Mutual Funds only. PruSec presents a fairly detailed profile of each of their funds. You can request a free prospectus on any fund by e-mail. Shareholder Services describes the services provided to purchasers of Prudential funds.

Glossary This is a fairly lengthy glossary of general investment terms.

Calculator This is another link to PruSec's Wealth Accumulation Calculator (generally known as a retirement calculator).

Financial Advisor Locator

This area has an interactive tool to help investors find the nearest PruSec Financial Advisor.

Prudential Online Gateway

This area is for people who already have accounts with PruSec. Although you cannot trade online, you can access account information that is updated daily and send e-mail to your broker.

Events and Seminars

Choose this from the Click and Pull Down menu to find out about upcoming free seminars.

Netwise Tidbit

League of American Investors
http://investorsleague.com

Relax. Play a game. It's free, it's easy, you can play the stock market and not lose a dime (or make a dime, but hey, it's only a game).

Quote.com

http://www.quote.com

Power Index Categories	
52 Week High & Low	Mutual Fund Searches
Biggest Gainer/Loser Lists	Mutual Fund Strategies
Charts	New High/Low Lists
Charts - Daily	News
Charts - Intraday	News By Company
Charts - Monthly	Offline Information
Charts - Weekly	Options Information
Dividends Per Share	Portfolio Price Alarms By E-mail
Earnings Per Share	Portfolio Updates By E-mail
Fundamental Stock Information	Portfolio/Watch List Tracking
Getting Started	P/E Ratio
Graphs (see also Charts)	Quicken-Compatible Information
Market Indicators	Quotes
Most Active Lists	Quotes - Bid & Ask
Mutual Fund Holdings	Quotes - Day's High & Low
Mutual Fund Information	Quotes - Volume
Mutual Fund News	Symbol Searches
Mutual Fund Performance Leader Lists	Volume Alert Lists
Mutual Fund Profiles	Watch List/Portfolio Tracking

Good charting and excellent mutual fund information can be found here. If you just want some quick info and you don't want to register (which can take a couple of days to take effect), bookmark the free quote screen on your browser (http://fast.quote.com/fq/quotecom/quote). This page does not require a login and provides access to: quotes, intraday and historical charts, ticker search, news headlines by company, portfolio tracking and market information such as Biggest Gainers and Most Actives.

Registration is required to view some additional free information. If you do register, Quote.com will send you an activation key by e-mail. Sometimes Quote.com's site takes a while to update its list of new registrants, so you may have to wait a day or two before your activation key will be accepted.

Get Free Quotes

You can enter several symbols at once, separated by spaces.

The quote will provide:

- date and time (of the last trade)
- opening price, high and low
- last
- change in price
- volume
- earnings per share
- price/earnings ratio
- dividends per share
- the 52-week price range

Clicking on a symbol will bring up related news headlines.

Quotes (once you've registered)

Once you've registered, a different quote screen is available. This upgraded quote additionally provides:

- Bid & Ask
- several of the most recent sale priccs
- number of Ticks (sales)

You will also be able to select a format for the quotes. HTML (the format for viewing with your browser) is standard, but Quicken, YYMMDD and Quicken7 formats are also available.

News Headlines

Clicking on the News Headlines button in the quote screen will provide you with recent headlines relating to the company. Reading the full text of the articles requires buying a subscription from Quote.com. Even so, knowing about the headline (and the specific date and time it was released) can be helpful in tracking the movement of a stock. Remember also that full-text stories are available at other web sites such as My Yahoo!

Charts

Charts are available from the quote drop-down menu:

- 1-Minute Chart
- 5-Minute Chart
- Daily Chart
- Weekly Chart
- Monthly Chart

Industry Groups

Choosing Industry Groups from the quote menu leads to a menu of market information that goes beyond just industry groups.

The Industry Groups section provides quote tables on groups of stocks in specific industries, with individual quotes and brief business descriptions, as well as index quote and movement information. The following industry groups are profiled:

- Internet Stocks
- Computers (PCs)
- Airlines and Aircraft
- Biotechnology
- Leisure Products
- Consumer Electronics
- Computers (Workstation)
- Computers (Networking)
- Computer Software

In the Stock Markets section, Top 10 lists are provided from the three big exchanges for:

- Most Actives
- Biggest Gainers
- High Alerts
- Low Alerts
- Biggest Losers
- Volume Alerts
- 52-wk Highs
- 52-wk Lows

Intraday Charts provides graphic representations for the following market indicators:

- Dow Jones 30 Industrial Average ($INDU)
- S & P 500 Index ($INX)
- S & P 100 Index ($OEX)
- NASDAQ Composite Index ($COMPX)

Index and Forex, meanwhile, present quote tables of the major market indices, the Dow Industrials and the exchange rates for the major foreign currencies.

Mutual Funds

Search on a fund symbol or name to review free in-depth information on funds.

Lipper Analytical's reports provide:

- NAV (current quote)
- NAV change
- Offer price
- Investment Category
- Total Net Assets
- Yield

- Volatility
- Beta
- Performance over the last 1 week, 26 weeks, Year to date, 1 year, 3 years, 5 years, 10 years
- Performance since inception
- Total Return over the last 3, 5 and 10 years
- Total Return since inception
- Quintile Rank over the last 1, 3 and 5 years
- Numeric Rank over the last 1, 3 and 5 years
- Figures for the Universal Performance Quintile (Current, Up and Down)
- Minimum Investment required
- maximum sales charge
- redemption fee
- expense ratio
- 12b-1 Fee
- Income Dividends
- Capital Gains Dividends
- Distribution Frequency
- whether the fund has a periodic investment plan
- whether the fund has a systematic withdrawal plan
- manager's name and amount of time served
- Fund Family
- Phone number
- Asset Valuation (percentage of fund's assets in Cash, Stocks, Convertible Securities, Fixed Income Securities and Other investments)
- Percentage of holdings in each industry sector (such as Technology, Consumer Cyclical)
- Some of the stocks held by the fund

Morningstar reports provide similar information, and also notably provides a Morningstar Rating, Morningstar Risk Rating, Morningstar Return Rating and brief narrative description of each fund.

- Performance for year to date, and the last 3 months, 1, 3, 5 and 10 year returns
- Fund Family
- Manager Name, Tenure and Date Started
- Phone number
- Front Load
- 12b-1 Fee
- Deferred Sales Charge
- Minimum Initial Purchase
- Redemption Fee

- Expense Ratio
- Portfolio Composition (Cash, Stocks, Bonds, Other)
- Price/Earnings Ratio of Portfolio
- Price/Book Ratio of Portfolio
- Median Market Capitalization of Portfolio
- Sector Weightings

Top Performer lists are available from both Morningstar and Lipper ranking returns over the last 1, 3, 5 and 10 years.

Mutual Fund Screening is a sophisticated screening tool that allows you to search for funds meeting requirements you set yourself from a relatively long list of fund characteristics. In addition, you can create up to 4 different screens and have Quote.com run the screens periodically and e-mail the results to you.

Mutual Fund Tutorial provides and in-depth introduction to funds, and includes a mutual fund glossary. Articles are under the broad topics of:

- What Is A Mutual Fund?
- Getting Started With Mutual Funds
- Choosing A Fund
- Types Of Mutual Funds
- Managing And Monitoring Your Mutual Fund

Portfolio

From the free quote screen, click on portfolio in the menu bar at the top of the page. The General Quotes view provides:

- Time of last sale
- Open
- High
- Low
- Last
- Change
- Volume

The Profit/Loss portfolio view provides:

- Purchase date
- Number of shares
- Purchase price
- Total value at purchase
- Current price
- Current value
- Profit or loss per share
- Total profit or loss

The Fundamentals portfolio view shows:

- Name
- Earnings Per Share
- P/E ratio
- Dividends Per Share
- 52-week Price Range

Options

Options quotes are available, but you must know the option type, expiration, and strike price in order to obtain a quote.

Annual Reports (offline)

Annual Reports from about 3000 companies can be ordered from this area of the site, and each report will be sent to you by mail.

Bank Rates

This area offers information and rates for Online Banking & Trading, Credit Markets and Money Markets.

Netwise Tidbit

Combat Trading

http://www.inforel.com/~combat

Free daily information for the fully-hyphenated: hard-core risk-tolerant day-traders only.

Regal Discount Securities

http://www.regaldiscount.com

Power Index Categories	
Articles	Quotes - Bid & Ask
Brokers	Quotes - Day's High & Low
Getting Started	Quotes - Volume
Investment Strategies	Stock Ideas
Newsletters	Symbol Searches
Quotes	

This site does not offer a great deal in terms of free information, but its articles on investment strategies are well worth reading.

Rewarding Times

This is Regal's electronic magazine on investing. Look under Basic Trading Strategies for an informative article entitled 5 Simple Rules to Making & Keeping Profits. This is not a stock-picking strategy, but rather a stock-selling strategy.

Once you know when to sell, you still have to figure out what to buy. You'll find a section on Scouting Out Great Stocks with ideas on how to do it. Under Advice From The Authors, you'll find specific stock ideas; they'll also tell you how their previous recommendations have done.

Each issue also has new articles on varying topics. Some of the articles are designed to educate you on the issues of dealing with brokers. Keep in mind when you read these that this online magazine is published by one of these brokers that is competing for your business. There are also articles highlighting certain market sectors, such as the solid waste industry. If you don't see what you want in the latest issue, take a look at the Archive of old articles.

Quotes

Delayed quotes are provided by StockCenter, and include:

- Price
- Change
- High
- Low
- Volume
- Bid & Ask

Symbol search is available.

Research Magazine/InvestorNet

http://www.researchmag.com

Power Index Categories	
Premier Site	Net Profit Margin
52 Week High & Low	News
ADR (American Depositary Receipts) Information	News By Company
Articles	Personal Finance
Charts	Phone Numbers of Companies
Charts - Weekly	Portfolio/Watch List Tracking
Company Profiles	P/E Ratio
Dividends Per Share	Quicken-Compatible Information
Earnings Information	Quotes
Earnings Per Share	Quotes - Day's High & Low
Financial Planning	Quotes - Volume
Fundamental Stock Information	Resistance
Getting Started	Retirement Planning
Global Investment & Economic Information	Revenue
Graphs (see also Charts)	Sales Per Share
International Investment Information	Stock Predictions
Investment Club Information	Stock Ideas
Investor Relations Contacts	Stocks - Searching by Technical Criteria
Mutual Fund Information	Support
Mutual Fund Performance Leader Lists	Symbol Searches
Mutual Fund Profiles	Technical Evaluations / Predictions by Stock
Mutual Fund Searches	Technical Screening Tools
Net Income	Wall Street Analysis of Stocks
	Watch List/Portfolio Tracking
	Worksheets - Retirement Needs

This is one of the best investment sites on the web. Go directly into InvestorNet, which is designed specifically for the private investor. To use the site's excellent portfolio tracking tool, you'll have to register and choose a username and password. Registration requires providing your name, address, phone number and e-mail address.

Also of special interest are the charts, which provide resistance and support figures, as well as predictions of the stock's future movements. The Stock Summary screens provide Revenue and Income figures; you can also determine a company's Net Profit Margin using this information (see below).

InvestorNet's main menu lays out its wide variety of information resources.

Getting Started

The name says it all. Topics include:

- Investing 101
- What Every Investor Should Know
- Invest Wisely
- How's Your Portfolio Doing? Ways to Help Figure it Out

There is also a Glossary of investment terms.

Quotes

Quotes are free on a 20 minute delay during market hours. You can request a number of quotes at once, or search on a company name. (If you only need information on one company at a time, you can use Go To Ticker from the InvestorNet homepage as well.) Quotes provide:

- the last trade price
- change

Click on the ticker symbol in the quote table to view:

- current price
- high
- low
- change
- volume
- business description

Below the expanded quote chart mentioned above, you'll find links to:

- Investor News
- Stock Summary
- Stock Charts

Follow the Stock Summary link for information on revenues, income, earnings per share and dividends, as well as a chart with technical information.

Stock Summary

You can get to a Stock Summary through the Quote or Go To Ticker links. Stock Summary provides earnings and technical information:

- Price
- Previous close
- Open
- Change
- Volume
- Day's High & Low
- 52-Week High & Low
- Dividend Amount
- P/E Ratio
- Earnings Per Share
- Revenues for the last 2 quarters (and % change)
- Net Income for the last 2 quarters (and % change)
- Earnings per Share for the last 2 quarters (and % change)
- Wall Street Analysts' consensus earnings estimate for last quarter (to compare with actual earnings per share)
- Past several years of data on revenues, net income, earnings per share and dividends
- Current news headlines (if any)
- Link to More News Available, including company press releases
- 52-week price chart, including technical information on support and resistance figures, and a technical analysis of where the stock is headed in the short, medium and long term

Net Profit Margin as a percentage can also be determined using this information. For any year in the Stock Summary chart of earnings, use the following formula:

$$\frac{NetIncome}{Revenues} \times 100 = Net\,ProfitMargin\,\%$$

Charts

To get a chart, enter the ticker symbol and hit Go To Ticker from the InvestorNet homepage, then click on the Stock Charts button (the same chart appears in the Stock Summary page as well). The webmasters here have a Model-T philosophy when it comes to charts: you can have any chart you want, as long as it's a 52-week price history chart. On the other hand, the one chart you will get also has a section showing price ranges for the last 6 years.

Even nicer is the Technical Evaluation section on each chart that provides a prediction of the stock's prospects for the short, medium and long term. The Technical Evaluation section of the chart also provides Support and Resistance figures.

Featured Companies

For a certain number of companies, more in-depth information is available. Company profiles available in this area read like investor information brochures provided by the companies themselves.

Shareholder News

Press releases are available for select companies.

Stocks

Choose Stock Screens to search for stocks using criteria that you select (allowing you to "screen" a list of available stocks for those that match your requirements). You get to choose from characteristics such as:

- price range
- P/E range
- 5 Year Earnings Growth
- Current Dividend Yield
- Market Cap
- Average of Analyst Opinion
- Analyst EPS Estimates

Choose as many or as few criteria as you wish for your initial search. You'll be required to narrow your requirements until the search comes up with less than 100 companies matching your criteria. Once your results are listed, you'll be able to link to the following information (if available):

- Company Profile
- Shareholder News
- Wall Street Analysis
- Quick Stats
- 52-Week Chart

Ticker Search allows you to search for a company by entering part of the company name.

Sample Reports will give you access to extensive reports on about a dozen companies. The catch is that you don't get to choose which companies to look at, so this is only helpful if you're browsing for stock ideas. The reports are in PDF format, so you'll need Adobe's Acrobat Reader to view them (available free from http://www.adobe.com).

Funds

Featured Funds Funds from about a dozen companies are featured. For each fund, a detailed report is provided.

Fund Articles Posted here are some articles on mutual funds from Research: Magazine.

FundFinder This is basically an expanded symbol search engine for funds. Enter a company name, or symbol, or choose from a list of fund objectives, and FundFinder will execute the search.

Top Performing Funds This is Research's monthly list of top-performing mutual funds, listed by market sector. For each fund they provide:

- 1 month % gain
- 1 year return
- NAV
- Assets in Millions
- % Load
- Minimum First and Repeat Investments
- the company's phone number

Fund Screens Use this tool to screen for funds with a wide variety of basic, advanced and professional characteristics. Remember to fill in the blanks for a characteristic and check off the box to the left to include the characteristic in your search. You must narrow your search until less than 100 funds are returned as a search result. Once you obtain the names of specific funds, you will have to do more in-depth research on those funds elsewhere, since accessing Research's mutual fund reports require a paying subscription.

Global Investing

This section will explain investing in foreign companies using ADRs (American Depositary Receipts). ADRs are negotiable certificates that usually represent a company's publicly traded equity or debt. ADRs allow you to buy stock that trades on a foreign exchange, but get quotes and dividends in U.S. dollars. This section includes a directory of ADRs provided by the Bank of New York.

Portfolio

Research provides a simple and effective portfolio tracking tool that should satisfy most investors' needs for both a portfolio tracker and a watch list. You'll have to register and get a username and password to use your portfolio. You can keep track of several portfolios at once (for example, multiple brokerage accounts or a brokerage account and real estate assets). You will also be able to see subtotals and a grand total for your portfolios. Research will also provide portfolio information in Quicken-compatible format.

For each portfolio item, you enter: the ticker symbol; the number of shares; the total cost; and the purchase date.

Then whenever you access your portfolio, for each item you've entered you'll be provided with:

- Ticker
- Description/Company Name
- Number of Shares Held
- Purchase Price per share
- Total Cost
- Current Price
- Current Value
- Total Change
- Percentage Change

For each portfolio, you'll also get a subtotal of Total Cost, Current Value, Total Change and Percentage Change.

Clicking on the ticker symbol of a portfolio item will take you to the single quote screen for that symbol. From there you can access the Stock Summary and Stock Chart for that item.

Click on Portfolio Prices to see a view of your portfolio providing the following for each item:

- 52-Week High
- 52-Week Low
- Dividend Amount
- P/E Ratio
- Volume
- Previous Close
- Last
- Change in price

Portfolio Analysis allows you to analyze a portfolio, watch list or new group of stocks by a number of factors:

Percent Under 52 Week High
Percent Over 52 Week Low
Price % Change in 12 Months
Return on Equity
10K Value After Five Years
Debt/Equity Ratio
(Growth + Dividend Yield) / P/E Ratio
Market Value / Sales
Price/Earnings Ratio
Dividend Yield
Market Capitalization

Analyst Recommendation (AQO)
AQO % Change in 3 Months
EPS Estimate % Change in One Month
Number of Analysts Covering
Industry Sector

ALERTS will display the stocks in your portfolio and draw your attention to any change greater than 3% (up or down).

Expert Picks leads to a list of portfolios designed by various experts in the financial world at the beginning of the year. Check to see who picked what, and how it worked out.

Ticker Tape

For anyone with a Java-enabled browser, the Ticker Tape will open a separate window that allows you to review constantly updated quotes of your portfolio while using your regular browser window to visit other web sites. Running your cursor over the ticker screen just below the scrolling numbers will display a menu to speed up or slow down the pace of the ticker.

NAIC

Here you'll find information on the National Association of Investors Corporation (whose own web site is reviewed in this book as well). NAIC Featured Companies is a good place to look for fresh investment ideas.

Research: Magazine

This online magazine has articles of interest to both brokers and investors.

Retirement Planning

Make sure to read Eight Common Mistakes in Retirement Planning. The Retirement Zone provides a worksheet to help you understand your retirement needs (this is not a calculator - you have to do the math for yourself), as well as a checklist for your Countdown To Retirement.

Industry Spotlight

Articles posted here are from Research's magazine, and relate to various industry sectors. Analysts' Buy Recommendations are also provided for some sectors - but be sure and check the dates of the recommendations since they might be quite old.

Today's News

This area, accessible through a link at the bottom of the InvestorNet homepage, provides a morning and afternoon edition of financial news headlines.

Reuters MoneyNet.com

http://www.moneynet.com

Power Index Categories	
52 Week High & Low	News By Company
Advance/Decline Numbers	P/E Ratio
Charts	Portfolio/Watch List Tracking
Charts - Daily	Portfolio Updates By E-mail
Charts - Moving Average Lines	Quotes
Charts - Weekly	Quotes - Day's High & Low
Earnings Per Share	Quotes - Option Symbol
Economic Reports	Quotes - Volume
Graphs (see also Charts)	Software Downloads
Market Indicators	Watch List/Portfolio Tracking
News	

News, news, and more news (what did you expect from Reuters), with quotes and graphs thrown in to boot. The downloadable ticker program is for serious tinkerers only.

Business Headlines

Business headlines on the homepage link directly to the full text stories.

Market in Brief

This section, also on the homepage, provides a brief update on the Dow, NASDAQ and S&P 500, as well as Advance/Decline numbers and volume for the New York Stock Exchange.

Ticker Download

Reuters offers a free ticker program that you can download and use to track your portfolio during the day with a free delayed-quote feed from Reuters. The Ticker program allows you to set price alarm levels to warn of steep price increases or drops.

Quotes

Quotes provide:

- Price
- Change
- Volume

Click on the symbol in a quote screen to view an expanded quote with:

- Price
- Change
- Percentage Change
- Volume
- Daily High & Low
- Daily Open
- Previous Close
- 52-Week High & Low
- Price/Earnings Ratio
- Earnings Per Share
- Date & Time of quoted sale

Click on the Chart icon in the quote screen to view a 100 day chart with volume information. From this screen you can plot a weekly chart of the last 1, 2 or 5 years, or a daily chart of the last 50, 100, 250 or 500 trading days. Each chart also displays both a 50 and 200-day moving average line.

Click on News from the quote screen to view headlines (plus full-text stories) from Reuters as well as other news sources.

Option Chains

Enter a symbol and select paramaters such as the Strike Price Range and whether you want to display Puts or Calls, and a chart will show all options for the symbol, with:

- Strike
- Last Trade
- Net Change
- Volume
- Open Interest
- Daily High & Low
- Date (of the option)

Click on one of the symbols in the quote screen to view an additional screen for that symbol that will provide the actual option symbol (in case you want to obtain an options quote on that single option later), and the previous day's close. Once you have the specific option symbol, you can use the Options Quotes link to obtain a single quote.

Portfolio Tracker

Before you can use the tracker, you must register and then sign up for the tracker; both are free. The portfolio will provide the current value of the portfolio, but does not record the purchase price (or the price at the time you started watching the security), so you will not be able to see net profit or loss.

The portfolio can track stocks, mutual funds, call options and put options. You can also create more than one portfolio.

When you choose View E-Mail Schedule, you will have the opportunity to change the frequency with which Reuters will send you e-mail updates on your portfolios. Reuters considerately makes the default "none," but you can change that to daily, weekly or monthly, and also choose to receive the updates at mid-day or market close.

Company News

This will get you directly to news on a specific company (from Reuters and other news sources) without having to maneuver through the quote screens.

Price History (Graphs)

This is a short cut to the graph menu, avoiding the quote screens.

Market Snapshot

The default version of this page contains a serious overview of the markets, as described below. You can also customize this page to fit your needs.

Intraday Graphs displays the days ups and downs for the Dow Jones Industrials, the NAS/NMS Composite and the AMEX Composite.

Indices provides the last figure, change and percentage change for the Dow, the S&P 500 and the Internet Index.

The Statistics section displays important numbers for the NYSE, NASDAQ and AMEX:

- Advancing Issues
- Declining Issues
- Unchanging Issues
- Advancing Volume
- Declining Volume
- Unchanging Volume
- Total Volume
- New Highs
- New Lows

Headlines are all business-related, with full stories accessible with a click.

Commentaries provides intraday market commentary headlines (plus full stories with a click). The most recent stories are at the top.

Economic Reports focuses on economic indicators such as jobless claims and auto sales.

Charles Schwab & Co., Inc.

http://www.schwab.com

Power Index Categories	
52 Week High & Low	Mutual Fund Information
Brokers	Mutual Fund Performance Leader Lists
Brokers - Internet Trading	Mutual Fund Profiles
Charts	P/E Ratio
Charts - Daily	Quotes
Charts - Intraday	Quotes - Bid & Ask
Charts - Weekly	Quotes - Day's High & Low
Dividends Per Share	Quotes - Volume
Earnings Per Share	
Graphs (see also Charts)	

Schwab is a big player in the brokerage industry whether you're online or offline. Here they offer a general smattering of free quotes and charts, plus mutual fund information.

Brokerage Fees

Schwab offers online trading for $29.95 per trade up to 1000 shares.

Research

From the Delayed Quotes and Charts screen, a delayed quote will provide:

- last price
- net change
- day's high & low
- bid & ask
- last trade tick
- volume
- 52-week high & low
- earnings per share
- P/E ratio
- dividend

You can also choose from intraday, daily and weekly charts. Symbol search is available.

Mutual Fund OneSource Online

Check here for profiles of all of the mutual funds that can be purchased through Schwab.

Compare Top Performers at Schwab allows you to search the funds offered by Schwab for the top 10, 25 or 50 funds. You can search all funds or select a single investment category, and you get results over the last 3 months, 1 year, 5 years or 10 years.

Schwab's Select List lets you search among a shorter list of historically high-performing funds. The list is a cooperative effort by Schwab and Morningstar.

Custom Fund Search is not so much a fund search as it is a performance comparison tool. Enter two or more mutual fund symbols, and you will be able to make a side by side comparison (well, above and below comparison, anyway) of the funds' performance.

Netwise Tidbit

The Noble Group
http://www.experts.com

Frank Armstrong, author of *Investment Strategies for the 21st Century*, picks one investor's question a week to answer.

Stock Club

http://stockclub.com

Power Index Categories	
Brokers - Information	Rumors
Discussion Forums	Stock Predictions
Discussion Forums By Stock	Stock Ideas
Getting Started	

Stock Club features interactive discussion forums on individual stocks and other investment topics such as:

- short-term trading ideas
- buy-and-hold ideas
- under-$5 ideas

Entering any of the forums requires that you become a member, which is free. You'll have to provide at least your name and e-mail address, and choose a username and password. They promise not to sell or rent your name to anyone.

Remember that rumors abound in discussion forums. Always approach any information you find with a healthy dose of skepticism.

Stock Forums

There are forums for a large number of individual stocks. And if you don't find a forum for your stock, you can Create a stock forum now. Stocks are listed alphabetically (by name and by symbol), as well as by industry groups.

Broad Topics

General investment topics are discussed in the forums found here, including:

- Day-Trading Techniques
- Free-for-All
- Online Brokerages

stockprofiles.com

http://www.stockprofiles.com

Power Index Categories	
12-Month Earnings	Earnings Report Dates by Company
52 Week High & Low	Float
Addresses of Companies	Fundamental Stock Information
Annual Dividend	Market Cap
Annual Report Dates by Company	Number of Shares
Average Daily Volume	Phone Numbers of Companies
Beta	Price/Book
Book Value	P/E Ratio
Cash Per Share	Quotes
Company Profiles	Return on Assets
Current Ratio	Return on Equity
Dividend Yield	Sales Per Share
Dividends Per Share	Shares Outstanding
Earnings Information	Symbol Searches
Earnings Per Share	Total Debt/Equity

The Snapshot reports offered here are an excellent source of fundamental information on companies.

Snapshot

This area contains snapshot reports on most companies you'll be interested in following (including NASDAQ Small Cap stocks), with substantial fundamental information. Search either by name or ticker symbol. Snapshots provide the following information:

- address and phone number
- Sector group
- Industry Group
- Date that Complete Financials will be released
- Date that Earnings Announcements are expected
- a Business Summary including earnings information
- the latest Earnings Announcement, if available
- 52 Week High
- 52 Week Low
- 3 Month Average Daily Volume
- Beta

- Market Cap
- Shares Outstanding
- Float
- Indicated Annual Dividend
- Dividend Yield
- Earnings Per Share
- P/E Ratio
- Book Value
- Price/Book
- Sales Per Share
- Return on Assets
- Return on Equity
- Cash Per Share
- Current Ratio
- Total Debt/Equity

Featured Companies

There were about 50 companies listed here when we visited, and most of them were traded on the NASDAQ exchange. Some linked to the individual company's own web sites, while other profiles were within the stockprofiles site. Expect a profile to tell you a little about what each company does and its competition.

Annual Reports

Only a few annual reports are available here.

Stock Quotes

Quotes are provided via a link to Quote.com (see this book's review of Quote.com for details).

Netwise Tidbit

NetTax '9X

http://www.nettax.com

Free online U.S. tax calculation program and Form 1040 preparation aid.

Taxing Times

http://www.scubed.com/tax/index.html

Power Index Categories	
Tax Code (Federal)	Tax Information
Tax Forms	

A bunch of employees at a company called Maxwell Labs apparently noticed that they had at least one thing in common: they all filed taxes. So they got together and dumped as much tax information and forms as possible onto their web site.

Federal Forms and Instructions

Now that the IRS is online, this site simply offers you a link to the IRS site for downloading forms. However, there is information here that should be reviewed before dealing with the IRS. There is a description of Tele-Tax, the IRS' automated tax assistance service, and advice on how to deal with the IRS by phone, including a list of the IRS' Toll-Free Tax Help Telephone Numbers.

State Forms and Instructions

Not every state is covered, but they do provide links to a number of state's tax web sites.

Tax Code

Yes, the entire tax code (courtesy of MIT), but it's not necessarily the most recent one, so use it as a starting point only for complicated questions.

IRS Code and Subject Telephone Directory

Those delving deep into the meaning of the tax code will find treasure in this list of the name and phone number of the IRS officer assigned to each Intenal Revenue Code section. The list is provided by TimeValue Software (http://www.timevalue.com).

TenPlus

http://www.iistenplus.com

Power Index Categories	
Free Trials	Options Trading Ideas
Options Information	Stock Ideas

This is a pay service whose investment strategy includes selling options on stock you own to generate additional income (of course, they want you to pay them to help find the best stock/option combination opportunities).

There are 2 opportunities here for the thrifty investor. First, scroll down the homepage and read the info-article that will introduce you to a lot of the terms involved in options. Second, you can sign up for their free trial. To register, you must provide your name, address, phone number and e-mail address.

Netwise Tidbit

The Rogue Market

http://www.roguemarket.com

If you're tired of trading stock in companies, try this free stock market game that trades shares in public figures instead.

T. Rowe Price

http://www.troweprice.com

Power Index Categories	
Articles	Market Commentary
Bond Information	Mutual Fund Companies
Brokers	Mutual Fund Information
Calculators - Retirement	Offline Information
Getting Started	Portfolio/Watch List Tracking
Global Investment & Economic Information	Quicken-Compatible Information
International Investment Information	Quotes
Investment Strategies	Retirement Planning
IRA Information	Risk Tolerance
Market Analysis	Tax Information
	Watch List/Portfolio Tracking

T. Rowe Price is a mutual fund company and discount brokerage (they did not offer internet stock trading at the time of review). If you're not interested in their mutual funds, you might still want to take a look at their T. Rowe Price Insights Library for it's general overview of investing principles and strategies.

What's News

Daily Market Updates This links you to DBC Online for quotes, personal portfolio setup and other market information. Check out this book's summary of DBC Online for a complete breakdown of the information available here.

Fixed Income Markets This is a weekly update of the bond market, with narratives on the treasury market, the corporate market, mortgage-backed securities and municipal bonds.

Credit Market Comments This will give you a big picture view of where the economy's heading.

T. Rowe Price Market Viewpoint Recent and not-so-recent articles are posted here, along with a few sales pitches. Samples include Update on Technology Stocks, and A Word on Market Corrections.

Equity Market Updates & International Market Summaries These provide weekly narratives of happenings in the stock markets in the U.S. and around the world.

Retirement Planning

Get Started by taking a look at common sources of retirement income and why starting early can make a big difference. You'll find explanations of individual options such as IRAs, Rollover IRAs and Variable Annuities, as well as retirement plans for small businesses such as SEP and Keogh Plans, and 401(k) Plans.

Follow How much to save and try out the Retirement Planning Worksheet (which is actually a retirement calculator that will do the math for you). You can also order the T. Rowe Price Retirement Planning Kit by mail (or a software version by phone: 1-800-541-4041). If you're currently in retirement or close to it, you can also order the offline Retirees Financial Guide. If you think you already know enough about this stuff, take the Quiz just to make sure.

Mutual Fund Information

Start with Getting Started: Investing with Mutual Funds for a tutorial on defining your goals, determining your risk tolerance and finding a fund to match your objectives (but don't be surprised if T. Rowe Price conveniently has a fund that matches your objectives precisely).

Prices & Profiles End-of-day prices are available for all T. Rowe Price Funds. The prices can be downloaded in Quicken format if desired. The Fund Price and the Price Change are provided for each fund, and by clicking on the name of each fund, you can see a more complete profile of the fund including:

- the Net Assets
- the Portfolio Management Team
- Investment Objective, Strategy and Risk/Reward
- Investor Profile
- Fees and Charges
- Minimum Investment
- Significant Holdings

Performance Information Current and past performance figures for every T. Rowe Price fund are located here, updated daily.

T. Rowe Price Insights Library This is the site's best source of information for the new investor. Articles under General Information include:

- The ABC's of Investing
- Mutual Fund Investing
- Tax Information for Mutual Fund Investors

Under the Types of Securities heading you'll find articles including:

- The Basics of Tax-Free Investing
- Common Stock

- Global Bond Investing
- Investing in Emerging Growth Stocks
- Investing in Small-Company Stocks

Articles on Investment Strategies include:

- Conservative Stock Investing
- Dollar Cost Averaging
- Equity Index Investing
- Managing Risk Through Diversification
- The Power of Compounding

Investment Strategy Planner This will take you through defining your goals and time horizon, determining your risk tolerance, matching your goals with an investment strategy, and (of course) considering whether to implement your strategy with T. Rowe Price funds.

International Investing This area contains a number of features on international mutual fund investing. Take a look if you are interested in putting part of your portfolio in the international market. There is even an International/Domestic Mix Analyzer, a calculator to help you look at the potential return and volatility of investing internationally.

Watch List

If you like, you can register (for free) and create your own watch list of T. Rowe Price funds, updated on a daily basis.

Netwise Tidbit

Doubtful Accounts
http://
www.doubtfulaccounts.com
Stock market cartoons by Doug Pike.

Univ. of Missouri-St. Louis

http://anasazi.umsl.edu

Power Index Categories	
Articles	Investment Strategies
Getting Started	

You used to dream of sneaking out of class. Here's your chance to sneak back in. Drop in on the School of Business Administration and audit class number BA334 - Investments. The course's objective: "Obtain a working knowledge of investment techniques and skills as they are practiced in the industry."

Investment Readings

Click on Investment Readings, Overheads ... from the main page to see a list of articles that are great for any investor to read, including Peter Lynch's List of Stock Selection Tips.

Stock Information on Student Choices

In this area, you'll find links to a number of Zacks reports on various companies. Since some of the information in Zacks earnings reports are time sensitive, such as buy/sell recommendations, be sure to check the date on each report.

Netwise Tidbit

Internet Center for the Abused Investor

http://www.investoraid.com

When things go really bad, it may be time to call in the lawyers. This firm's site will answer some general questions about settling problems with brokers.

The Vanguard Group

http://www.vanguard.com

Power Index Categories	
Articles	Mutual Fund Companies
Asset Allocation	Mutual Fund Information
Calculators - Asset Allocation	Mutual Fund Profiles
Calculators - Investment Personality	Newsletters
Calculators - Retirement	Offline Information
Getting Started	Portfolio/Watch List Tracking
Glossaries	Retirement Planning
Glossaries - Mutual Fund Terms	Risk Tolerance
	Watch List/Portfolio Tracking

Vanguard is primarily a mutual fund company, and the main purpose of the site is to distribute information on Vanguard's own funds. The Investor Education area is a good place to start learning about mutual funds.

Investor Education

Enter the University for a series of articles (lectures?) on the fundamentals of mutual funds. The second series of articles in this section is an Introduction to Retirement Investing; take the Preview Quiz to see how much you already know and check out the Glossary of mutual fund terms here as well.

If you want to do additional research, you go to the Library, of course. Topics include:

- Retirement Investing
- Investing in the 1990's
- Mutual Funds & Taxes
- Emerging Markets Investing

And when you're ready to get your hands dirty, you drop in on the Laboratory. Custom Daily Fund Prices will allow you to track a custom portfolio (but only of Vanguard Funds), including:

- NAV
- NAV Change
- YTD Return
- 1 Year Return
- 5 Year Return
- 10 Year Return

While you're in the lab, check out the Retirement Calculator.

Vanguard Catalog

The Online Library features a number of articles, mostly on mutual funds but also on other topics such as tax-deferral and living trusts.

The Literature Library allows you to order Vanguard's brochures offline. The Vanguard Newsstand contains back issues of Vanguard's newsletters, including: In the Vanguard; MoneyWhys; and Market View.

Retirement Center

Follow Planning for Retirement and use their calculator to determine How much you should save for retirement.

How to Develop an Investment Strategy includes calculators to Determine Your Risk Tolerance as well as Determine Your Investment Mix (with suggestions on how to balance your portfolio between stocks, bonds and cash reserves).

Mutual Funds

Here Vanguard profiles each of the mutual funds they offer, providing:

- category
- risk
- asset type
- inception date
- expense ratio
- total assets
- minimum initial investment
- ticker symbol
- objective
- prospectus (read online or request by mail)
- Sector Diversification information
- performance information (compared to S&P 500 Index)
- management information

You can look at the funds alphabetically or by category, risk level or asset type.

Zacks

http://www.zacks.com

Power Index Categories	
Charts Company Profiles Earnings Estimates By Company Earnings Surprises By Company Earnings Surprises, Daily Graphs (see also Charts) Metastock-Compatible Information	Portfolio Updates By E-mail Quicken-Compatible Information Ranking In Industry By Company Stock Ideas Quotes Wall Street Analysis of Stocks

Start by entering the Individual Investors area, then on to Free Research.

Quotes and Charts

These are supplied by Quote.com (see the profile in this guide for details).

Portfolio Alert

This free service will send you a daily e-mail with quotes on up to ten stocks and mutual funds. The reports are available in a number of formats including Quicken and Metastock.

Public Companies

This area provides Zacks reports for a very short list of companies.

Historical Financial Tables

Though not all publicly traded companies are covered here, for featured companies Zacks provides the last several years of income statement data, including Net Sales, Gross Profit, Income after Depreciation & Amortization, Pretax Income, Income from Continuing Operations and the like.

Company Reports

Pop in any ticker symbol, and Zacks will tell you:

- the number of brokers following the stock, and what their recommendations are (from Strong Buy down to Strong Sell)
- the average broker recommendation (expressed as a number)

- the previous week's average broker recommendation
- the company's ranking within its industry
- Consensus estimate for current fiscal year
- Consensus estimate for next fiscal year
- Consensus estimate for current quarter
- Last quarter's actual earnings
- Last quarter's EPS Surprise

Earnings Surprises

This page provides a simple table of the day's extremely good and bad earnings surprises. For each company featured, you can see the actual earnings per share, the percentage amount the earnings differed from estimates, and the time the news was released.

Netwise Tidbit

Web Investors
http://www.webinvestors.com
A first-rate dictionary, plus other investors share their Scary Stories.

Index

Symbols

A

D

E

F

J

K

L

S

W

Y

Z